2 TIMOTHY
THE 3:16 SERIES

# FINISH-LINE FAITH

# MATT PROCTOR

CP PUBLISHING · JOPLIN, MISSOURI

*This book is dedicated to the memories*
*of my father-in-law **Don Bunton** and my grandfather **I.O. Weede***
*who both passed away during its writing.*
*Both were farmers, family men, faithful elders*
*who loved the Lord and encouraged me.*
*Both finished well.*

1959 ★ 2009

**COLLEGE**
—— P R E S S ——

Copyright © 2009
CP Publishing
A division of College Press Publishing Co.
3rd Printing 2010

Toll-free order line 800-289-3300
On the web at www.collegepress.com

**The 3:16 Series** (Colossians 3:16)
"Let the word of Christ dwell in you richly . . . ."

Cover design by Brett Lyerla
Interior design by Dan Rees

International Standard Book Number 978-0-89900-976-6

# THE 3:16 SERIES

The Apostle Paul encouraged Christians in the first century and therefore us today to **"let the Word of Christ dwell in you richly"** (Colossians 3:16, *NIV*).

The 3:16 Series is based on this verse in Colossians. The series is designed primarily for small group study and interaction but will also prove fruitful for individual study. Each participant is encouraged to read the chapter before the group's meeting. The interaction questions are designed to be the focal point of your group's discussion time.

Psalm 119:11 says, *"I have hidden Your Word in my heart that I might not sin against You."* One noteworthy feature of this series is that each study includes a suggested memory verse (a short verse or two from the passage that is being studied).

**"Let the Word of Christ . . . have the run of the house.
Give it plenty of room in your lives."**
(Col. 3:16 *The Message*)

# Previewing Our Study of 2 Timothy

## MATT PROCTOR

**Chapter One: When You Feel Like Giving In (2 Timothy 1:1-2)**

The race called the Christian life can be tough. Even when you start well, you can find yourself faltering before the race is over. You begin to doubt your ability to finish. Timothy was ministering to the church Paul started in Ephesus, but it was a tough assignment. Timothy was overwhelmed and felt like quitting. Like a coach, Paul gives a pep talk to Timothy that can encourage all of us to finish "the course marked out for us."

**Chapter Two: Remember Your Heritage (2 Timothy 1:3-5)**

"Like father, like son." Our family heritage influences each of us, and Timothy's primary influences while growing up were his godly mother and grandmother. Paul encourages Timothy to remember that upbringing and show the same continuing faithfulness. While you may not have a Christian family heritage, you can take encouragement from those in Scripture, from examples throughout church history, and from your own congregational and personal mentors.

**Chapter Three: Rely on the Spirit (2 Timothy 1:6-7)**

Wouldn't you like to have superhuman powers? Maybe flying and seeing through walls belong to the realm of fiction, but that doesn't mean you can't do more than you ever thought you could. Paul reminds Timothy, and thus reminds us, that we have access to the Holy Spirit's supernatural power to strengthen us for the race.

**Chapter Four: Meditate on the Gospel (2 Timothy 1:8-12)**

The longer we are in the faith, the easier it can be to forget how amazing the Good News is! Paul reminds Timothy of the facts of the gospel—

the grace for our past, the hope for our future, and the power for our present. Meditating on God's great gift will inspire you to continue following God's great call.

### Chapter Five: Guard the Truth (2 Timothy 1:13–2:2)

Guarding the Tomb of the Unknown Soldier is one of the highest honors a soldier can be given. According to Paul, Timothy's task of guarding the truth of the gospel was the highest of all duties. While Paul knew some who had betrayed the truth, he commends Onesiphorus for his sacrificial devotion and encourages Timothy to seek out others who would be able to pass the truth to still others, guarding it for generations to come.

### Chapter Six: Expect Tough Times (2 Timothy 2:3-13)

Soldiers, athletes, and farmers have one thing in common. They know that what they are doing is not easy, but they also know it is worth it. Timothy can carry on through the tough times because God is with him and makes it all worthwhile.

### Chapter Seven: Maintain Your Character (2 Timothy 2:14-26)

Previously Paul used three metaphors for dealing with difficult times. Now he uses three metaphors for dealing with difficult people while still maintaining a Christlike character. Like a trustworthy workman, Timothy must maintain his integrity. Like a noble instrument, Timothy must maintain his purity. Like a bondservant, Timothy must maintain his humility.

### Chapter Eight: Choose Wise Examples (2 Timothy 3:1-13)

Wherever God's truth is being proclaimed, Satan also has his false teachers. As Paul admonishes Timothy, we are to look to the right teachers and be on guard against those who would lead us astray. Avoid imitation Christianity, and look instead for Christianity worth imitating.

### Chapter Nine: Nourish Yourself on Scripture (2 Timothy 3:14-17)

The old saying that "you are what you eat" is true in a physical sense, but even more true in a mental and spiritual sense. Timothy had been fed as a child on the Holy Scriptures, and it was important for him to continue in them. If we nourish ourselves on the Word of Christ, we will begin to develop the character of Christ.

### Chapter Ten: Speak God's Message (2 Timothy 4:1-8)

Paul's final words to Timothy are compelling and clear: Preach the Word, at all times and under all circumstances. Timothy must not fail in this evangelistic task, because Paul is leaving and Christ is coming. The world is lost, the final judgment is soon, and Paul will no longer be around to preach. Timothy—and every Christian—is charged to be a messenger of the gospel.

### Chapter Eleven: Cultivate Real Community (2 Timothy 4:9-15,19-22)

Even though Paul's personal remarks at the end of his letter may seem irrelevant today, we can learn from them this lesson: the Christian life is never lived alone. Paul always sought out a "band of brothers" with whom he could share life. Timothy too must stay connected to fellow believers, for only in the church will he find a warm welcome, a second chance and a helping hand when things get tough.

### Conclusion: Stay Close to Jesus (2 Timothy 4:16-18)

In the last recorded moments of Paul's life, he gives a powerful testimony to Jesus' faithful presence. Even in his darkest hour, Christ is with him. If we want to finish well like Paul, we must stay close to Jesus. Then we too can go out with a testimony on our lips and a song in our hearts. That's finish-line faith!

# TABLE OF CONTENTS

# FINISH-LINE FAITH

# CHAPTER ONE

# WHEN YOU FEEL LIKE GIVING IN

## 2 TIMOTHY 1:1-2

*"I have fought the good fight. I have finished the race.
I have kept the faith."*

—Paul, in 2 Timothy 4:7

Question: If the Christian life is a race, have you ever felt like quitting?

Every time I read 2 Timothy 4:7, I think of Big Jake. Jake was a teammate on my high school track team. I ran long distance; Jake threw shot put. We called him Big Jake because he was, quite simply, massive. He'd been shaving since second grade (or so it seemed), and he had muscles in places where I didn't even have places.

However, Jake was not exactly the brightest candle on the cake. Case in point: Once our team was given an extra entry in the mile race, and Big Jake volunteered to run. We could not contain our surprise. He had never run *one* lap around the track, let alone the four laps that make a mile. But it was his senior year, and Jake wanted to go out in a blaze of glory. Coach gave him the spot.

The day came, the mile runners lined up, the gun fired, and to our astonishment, Big Jake took off like a deer . . . or more like a buffalo. He *sprinted* out around the first curve, opening a large lead. Like a locomotive with a full head of steam, he was chugging down the track. A blaze of glory indeed.

But something began to happen during the second lap. Big Jake started to slow. His stride was losing its strength, the pack of runners began to pass him, and it quickly became apparent: Big Jake had burned all his fuel in that spectacular launch. He was running on fumes. Soon he was in dead last.

He was in a world of pain. Every muscle in Big Jake's body (and there were a lot of them) was screaming for him to quit, and halfway around the last lap, he did just that. With a mighty sigh, he just stopped running. He bent over and grabbed his knees, fighting for air, and after a few moments to regain his balance, he walked slowly off the track. The blaze of glory had flickered out.

Big Jake never finished the race, and that day I marked down what you might call the Big Jake Principle: *It's not how you start the race that matters. It's how you finish.*

If the Christian life is a race, have you ever felt like quitting?

## A Difficult Life

After all, the Christian life is hard.

On my desk, I have a large red pushbutton with the word "easy" on it. Maybe you've seen the office supply store commercials that featured this button. Anytime you have a problem, the commercials told us, just push the "easy button" and all will be solved. Out of copy paper? Press the "easy button," and paper appears. Coworker playing obnoxious rap music? Press the "easy button," and he's listening to country-western.

Unfortunately, some Christians think this ought to be included in the gift of salvation. Wouldn't it be great if we were handed an "easy button" on our way out of the baptistery? One push and God would make all of our problems disappear. Hard time paying the bills? Press the "easy button," and your bank account is full. Difficult boss? Press the "easy button," and he's nicer than Mr. Rogers. Isn't that the way the Christian life is supposed to work?

A young man came into my office once, sat down, and began the conversation with these words: "I had no idea. For some reason, I really thought that when I became a Christian my troubles would go away. I didn't know that being a Christian was so hard."

My hunch is that you already know the Christian life is hard. You know because you've read your Bible. In John 16:33, Jesus says, "In this world, you will have trouble." In Acts 14:22, Paul says, "We must go through many hardships to enter the kingdom of God."

But it's not just Scripture's clear warnings that taught you to expect difficulty. Your own experience has taught you. You know the Christian life is hard because you've *lived* it:

- You've struggled to get free of a sinful habit that wouldn't let you go.
- You've ached through a painful church conflict that tore your congregation in half.
- You've lost a friend because she didn't understand why you took your new faith so seriously.
- You've prayed fervently for God to heal your father, but no miracle came, and he passed away.

You know there is no "easy button." Anyone who has followed Jesus for more than five minutes has experienced moments of defeat, fatigue, rejection, pain, and I'm wondering if you've ever been tempted to just stop. When you first became a Christian, still flush with gospel excitement, maybe you had visions of your new life as a constant blaze of glory. But you're a few laps into the race now, and perhaps the flame is flickering low. You're tempted to walk off the track and never come back.

If the Christian life is a race, have you ever felt like quitting?

## A Dear Son

Timothy did.

Who is this Timothy to whom the letter of 2 Timothy is addressed (1:1)? In a sentence, he was the apostle Paul's last earthly hope.

Second Timothy was written around A.D. 67, and some 15 years before, on a trip through the small town of Lystra, Paul met a young man whose spiritual maturity caught his attention. Timothy, perhaps 18 years of age or so, was "spoken well of by all the brothers," and seeing his kingdom potential, Paul invited Timothy to travel with him on the rest of his missionary journey (Acts 16:2-3).

The invitation proved to be life-changing for both men. Timothy had been raised under the godly influence of his mother Eunice and his grandmother Lois, but his father was not a believer and apparently not much on the scene. In Paul, Timothy found a spiritual father—someone who taught, encouraged, challenged, and cared deeply about him. For over a decade and a half, Timothy looked to Paul as a mentor and model, wisdom figure and hero.

In Timothy, Paul found the son he never had. In 1:2, when Paul calls Timothy "my dear son," the word *dear* is actually *agapeto*, or "beloved." You can hear the deep affection. While Paul taught Timothy as a rabbi would a disciple, Timothy was more than just another student. What began as a teacher/pupil relationship grew into a deep friendship. In 2 Timothy 1:4, Paul says, "I long to see you so that I may be filled with joy." In his New Testament letters, Paul mentions Timothy 18 times by name, and in Philippians 2:20, he even says, "I have no one else like him."

> In Paul, Timothy found a spiritual father who cared deeply about him.

Indeed, Paul entrusted to Timothy his most significant kingdom assignment—leading the church in Ephesus. Outside of Rome, Ephesus was the most strategic city in the Empire. Capital of the Roman province of Asia Minor, it stood at a major trade crossroads, at the midpoint of both the north-south and east-west travel across the Empire.

Large, diverse, and affluent, Ephesus was where Paul spent his longest recorded ministry. For three years, the apostle worked "night and day" to start and establish a healthy church in this premiere city, and when he left, he did not think he would ever return (Acts 20:25,31).

But now, years later, came disturbing news. To paraphrase the old song, Ephesus "starts with E and that rhymes with T and that stands for trouble." Along with the problems of materialism (1 Tim 6:5-10) and divisive attitudes (1 Tim 2:8), false teaching was threatening the church. These teachers, like wolves in sheepskin, were infiltrating the flock and leading many astray (1 Tim 1:19-20; 4:1-3; 2 Tim 2:17-18; 3:1-9; 4:3-4).

## A Difficult Assignment

Paul and Timothy returned to Ephesus to straighten out this mess, but after hearing of a pressing need in Macedonia, Paul decided to move on, leaving Timothy behind to set matters right (1 Tim 1:3). Now Timothy was alone with a big job on his hands. Forming a new church is hard work, but *reforming* an established church is even harder. Giving correction is always harder than giving direction.

*Giving correction is always harder than giving direction.*

To make matters worse, Timothy feels like he's stepping up to the plate with three strikes already against him. First, he's **young**. He was likely in his early 30s, and apparently the folks in the Ephesian church saw him as just another green Bible college kid, still wet behind the ears. In 1 Timothy 4:12, Paul hints that some are looking down on his youth. I once heard an older preacher jokingly say that to succeed in ministry you only needed two things: gray hair and hemorrhoids. He said the gray hair would make you look distinguished, and the hemorrhoids would make you look concerned! Timothy was ministering without the gray hair, and this young man got no respect. *Strike one.*

He was also **sickly**. If you've ever been on a trip in the developing world, what do they always tell you? "Don't drink the water." Apparently no one mentioned this to Timothy, so in 1 Timothy 5:23 Paul tells him, "Stop drinking only water," citing his "frequent stomach illnesses." Can you imagine: poor Timothy is preaching a sermon when he suddenly experiences an *Imodium A-D*™ moment. How embarrassing to have to make a quick exit! His weak constitution probably presented many challenges to fulfilling his ministry. *Strike two.*

To top it off, Timothy was something of an **introvert**. He was more inclined to stand on the sidelines than to get out on the field. That's why, in just four short chapters, Paul uses 35 imperatives in 2 Timothy. He sounds like a coach giving a pep talk! Listen to these "motivational moments" in Paul's letters to Timothy: "Don't neglect your gift . . . fight the good fight . . . fan into flame the gift of God which is in you . . . for God did not give us a spirit of timidity, but a spirit of power" (1 Tim 4:14; 6:12;

2 Tim 1:6,7). One scholar, John Stott, calls him "timid Timothy," and if that's true, then the thought of confronting misguided leaders would've made this soft-spoken young man inwardly cringe.[1]

*That's strike three, and Timothy wants outta there.* He's ready to be done with this ministry, throw in the towel, walk off the track, and never come back. If the Christian life is a race, he feels like quitting.

## A Determined Leader

So the apostle Paul picks up his pen.

Ephesus was too strategic, the false teaching too dangerous, Timothy's mission too important to let this situation go unaddressed.

By the way, here's an important note: Paul is especially urgent because he is writing this letter from prison. You might be thinking, "Yeah, so? Paul was, like, always in prison." Of course, you're right. Paul was what we would call a "repeat offender." Because of his bold preaching, Paul had compiled quite an arrest record, often spending time in the local lockup. As my friend Chris DeWelt says, "Paul was really into stocks and bonds."

But this time is different: Paul knows this is his last imprisonment. In just a few short months—or weeks—he will face execution. In 2 Timothy 4:6, Paul writes, "I am already being poured out like a drink offering, and the time has come for my departure." As one scholar puts it, 2 Timothy is written "in the shadow of the scaffold."[2]

Paul knows his death is imminent, and tragically, it appears that all his church planting in the province of Asia Minor has been for naught. At this time Nero was emperor, and Christians were his favorite scapegoat. Persecution loomed on the horizon, and to understate the case, it was an inconvenient time to follow Jesus. There was no "easy button," and consequently, 2 Timothy 1:15 describes an overwhelming exodus from these churches. "You know that everyone in the province of Asia has deserted me, including Phygelus and Hermogenes." Remember the parable of the sower in Mark 4? Like the seed in the rocky soil, these Asian believers had shallow roots. As Jesus had predicted, "When trouble or persecution comes because of the word, they quickly fall away" (Mark 4:17).

They weren't the last to ever fall away.

In his book *Finishing Strong*, Steve Farrar tells the story of John Bisagno, the long-time pastor of First Baptist Church in Houston:

> When John was just about to finish college, he was having dinner over at his fiancée's house one night. After supper, he was talking with his future father-in-law, Dr. Paul Beck, out on the porch. Dr. Beck had been in ministry for years, and that was inevitably the subject toward which the conversation turned.

"John, as you get ready to enter the ministry, I want to give you some advice," Dr. Beck told the younger man. "Stay true to Jesus! Make sure that you keep your heart close to Jesus every day. It's a long way from here to where you're going to go, and Satan's in no hurry to get you."

The older man continued, "It has been my observation that just one out of ten who start out in full-time service for the Lord at twenty-one are still on track by the age of sixty-five. They're shot down morally, they're shot down with discouragement, they're shot down with liberal theology, they get obsessed with making money . . . but for one reason or another nine out of ten fall out."

The twenty-year-old Bisagno was shocked.

"I just can't believe that!" he said. "That's impossible! That just can't be true."

Bisagno told how he went home, took one of those blank pages in the back of his Scofield Reference Bible and wrote down the names of twenty-four young men who were his peers and contemporaries. These were young men in their twenties who were sold out for Jesus Christ. They were trained for ministry and burning in their desire to be used by the Lord. These were the committed young preachers who would make an impact for the Lord in their generation.

Bisagno relates the following with a sigh: "I am now fifty-three years old. From time to time as the years have gone by, I've had to turn back to that page in my Bible and cross out a name. I wrote down those twenty-four names when I was just twenty years of age. Thirty-three years later, there are only *three names* remaining of the original twenty-four."[3]

I don't know how many names the apostle Paul had written in the back of his Bible, but he had just crossed out Phygelus and Hermogenes (2 Tim 1:15). Now there was only one name left: Timothy. All the other leaders on whom Paul was depending had abandoned the cause. As one commentator writes, "To every eye but that of faith it must have appeared just then as if the gospel were on the eve of extinction. . . . Christianity . . . trembled, *humanly speaking*, on the verge of annihilation."[4]

Timothy seemed like Paul's last earthly hope. He was depending on this young man, into whom he had poured his love and learning and life, to carry on his ministry. The torch of the gospel must be passed unquenched from one generation to the next, and Paul was determined that Timothy not fumble it. Timothy must grasp it firmly and hold it high. Paul needed Timothy to be the "one out of ten" to finish well.

The torch of the gospel must be passed unquenched from one generation to the next.

## A Divine Encouragement

So Paul picks up his pen and writes 2 Timothy, the last known letter from the apostle's hand. In this letter, he issues to Timothy essentially one charge: DON'T QUIT! Be faithful. Persevere. Endure. Don't give up. Don't give in. Keep running. Finish strong, Timothy! Stay on the track.

Paul is forging in Timothy what I call *finish-line faith*.

This letter is a powerful tool for shaping that kind of resilient faith. A priceless gift, these words from the aging apostle are better than any "easy button." Rather than simply removing hardship, these pages provide the wisdom needed to overcome hardship. These words shoot adrenaline through Timothy's weary soul.

In fact, as we begin our study of 2 Timothy, can I tell you the end of the story? The church historian Eusebius tells us that Timothy faithfully led the church in Ephesus for the next 30 years. In A.D. 97, after protesting the pagan festivities surrounding the worship of Artemis, he was finally stoned to death.

In other words, Timothy finished strong. This letter had done its work.

As you study 2 Timothy, I think you'll find new hope surging through your soul as well. When you feel like quitting the Christian life, this letter will send spiritual strength coursing through your veins.

It will equip you with finish-line faith.

How?

In the course of the four chapters of 2 Timothy, Paul will give instructions on how to go on when you feel like giving in—things like: remembering your heritage, meditating on the gospel, nourishing yourself on Scripture, and cultivating real community. You'll find his words to be straightforward, practical, and Spirit-inspired. They are exactly the divine encouragement a discouraged disciple needs.

In the next chapter, we'll begin our paragraph-by-paragraph study of 2 Timothy. Let me encourage you to read each biblical paragraph before you read the corresponding chapter in this book. God's Word is so powerful! In fact, as we close this chapter, read again Paul's first words to young Timothy. In 1:2, he writes, "Grace, mercy and peace from God the Father and Christ Jesus our Lord."

I know of a lady who decided to pray for a different friend each day for a year. Each morning she would write out her prayer on a postcard and send it, allowing that day's friend to "eavesdrop" at her prayer closet as she prayed for him or her. What an encouragement to listen in as one of God's saints intercedes on your behalf!

That's exactly what Paul is doing here for Timothy. Before the apostle moves into the body of his letter, he pauses to let Timothy overhear his prayers on Timothy's behalf. What does Paul pray for this disheartened young man? He asks for God to bestow three of his richest blessings: grace, mercy, and peace.

Don't miss the powerful message here. What is grace? It is God giving His attention to the undeserving. What is mercy? It is God giving His aid to the unable. What is peace? It is God giving His spiritual health to the unwell. That's a mighty prayer:

- Grace: God's worth to the worthless
- Mercy: God's help to the helpless
- Peace: God's rest to the restless[5]

As Timothy is allowed to eavesdrop at Paul's prayer closet, hearing him ask God to give these blessings, I'm sure Timothy draws great strength.

Here's the good news: these blessings are available to you too. God still gives His grace, mercy, and peace to those who ask, and it is still God our Father who enables His children to endure whatever hardships come their way.

What a simple but essential truth with which to begin this book: *God* gives us the strength to finish. While each study chapter will suggest a way to "go on when you feel like giving in," these suggestions are simply means of accessing the Father's resources. It is God—and God alone—who will bring us safely home. As the missionary Hudson Taylor once said, "It is not by trying to be faithful, but in looking to the Faithful One, that we win the victory." Or as the prophet Isaiah put it, "Those who wait upon the Lord shall renew their strength. They shall mount up with wings as eagles; they shall run and not grow weary . . ." (40:31, NASB).

With God's help, you can be the "one out of ten." Keep reading, and let Him forge in you a finish-line faith. Remember the Big Jake Principle: *it's not how you start the race that matters. It's how you finish.*

---

[1] John Stott, *The Message of 2 Timothy* (Downers Grove, IL: InterVarsity, 1973) 30.

[2] Donald Carson, Douglas Moo, and Leon Morris, *An Introduction to the New Testament* (Grand Rapids: Zondervan, 1992) 380.

[3] Steve Farrar, *Finishing Strong* (Sisters, OR: Multnomah, 1995) 16.

[4] Handley Moule, *The Second Epistle to Timothy* (Religious Tract Society, 1905) 16, 18.

[5] Adapted from John Stott, *The Message of 2 Timothy*, 26.

C
H
A
P
T
E
R

1 *When You Feel Like Giving In*

# Going On When We Feel Like Giving In

1. Describe something in your life which you didn't finish, but now wish you had—piano lessons, college, etc.

2. Answer the question: if the Christian life is a race, have you ever felt like quitting? If so, when and why? What were the circumstances? What helped you most in getting through the difficult time?

3. Did you expect the Christian life to be hard or easy? Explain. Do you know someone who has walked off the track as a believer? If so, why did they?

4. Timothy was young, physically sick, temperamentally shy, and had been given a difficult assignment. Are there ways in which you can identify with Timothy? How so?

5. What are the consequences of quitting? What are the rewards of finishing well?

6. Paul asked God to give Timothy three spiritual blessings. Which do you think you need the most? Take time to ask God for this blessing.
   - Grace: God's worth to the worthless
   - Mercy: God's help to the helpless
   - Peace: God's rest to the restless

*Paul, an apostle of Christ Jesus by the will of God, according to the promise of life that is in Christ Jesus, ²to Timothy, my dear son: Grace, mercy and peace from God the Father and Christ Jesus our Lord.*

CHAPTER TWO

# REMEMBER YOUR HERITAGE

## 2 TIMOTHY 1:3-5

*"What you have as heritage, take now as task;*
*for thus you will make it your own."*

—*Goethe*

The leadership of each generation is the legacy they leave to the next.

July 1, 1898. Cuba. Spanish-American War. At the bottom of San Juan Hill, Lt. Colonel Teddy Roosevelt prepared to lead the charge against 750 Spanish soldiers ordered to hold the heights. Just weeks before, he had resigned his commission as Assistant Secretary of the Navy to join the cavalry, saying, "I want to explain to my children someday why I did take part in the war, not why I didn't." So that July morning, Teddy strapped on his boots and led his Rough Riders regiment up the hill under fierce Spanish gunfire and on to victory. For his courage, he was eventually awarded the Congressional Medal of Honor.

June 6, 1944. Normandy, France. World War II. Sitting in the troop transport ships, Brigadier General Teddy Roosevelt, Jr., prepared to lead the attack on the most heavily fortified coast in history. Surely he was thinking of his father. President Roosevelt had poured his life into his four sons—telling them stories, teaching them horseback riding and how to handle a gun. When the Japanese ambassador visited the White House, President Roosevelt said, "Bring your sumo champions with you. I want my boys to learn how to wrestle." They wrestled in the living room of the White House! He instilled in those boys a passion for life, a sense of duty and a willingness to lead.

That's why Teddy Roosevelt Jr. was now preparing to lead the D-Day invasion. At first, his superiors had denied his request to go: "You're 57 years old. No other general is going ashore with the first wave of troops." But he insisted, "It will steady the men to know I'm with them." After his third request, they finally agreed. So that June morning, Teddy Jr. strapped on his boots and led the charge up the beach under fierce German gunfire and on to victory. For his courage, he was awarded the Congressional Medal of Honor . . . just like his father.

The leadership of each generation is the legacy they leave to the next.

When my wife Katie and I were preparing to celebrate ten years of marriage, we pulled out our wedding video to watch with our children. If you were to see our wedding video, you would be amazed at how slim and handsome I once was! My kids were certainly surprised. As she watched our exchange of vows, my five-year-old Lydia turned to me: "Daddy, you sure do look different there." Seven-year-old Luke replied matter-of-factly, "That's because he was young back then."

Luke was right. I was young. Twenty-one years old and immature, I didn't know the first thing about how to live well with another person, how to love my wife "as Christ loved the church." Ask my wife, and she'll tell you: that first year of marriage was hard. Tension, discouragement, conflict. As I watched the video, I thought, "What kept us going that year? How in the world did we make it?"

In the video, you can see Katie's Grandpa and Grandma Bunton. We were married on their 65th wedding anniversary. You can see both sets of my grandparents—each married for over 50 years. On the screen are Katie's parents, at that point married 41 years, and my parents with then-23 years of marriage.

That's how we made it: we'd been given a heritage of faithfulness. All those couples experienced hard times, but they worked their way through to the other side. We knew that's the way our families did things, and we knew we could do no less.

The leadership of each generation is the legacy they leave to the next.

## The Power of Remembering

Young Timothy wasn't sure he was going to make it. Overwhelmed and underappreciated in his ministry in Ephesus, Timothy felt like giving up. He was under fierce enemy fire and wondering, "Where will I find the courage to lead the charge?" In the opening paragraph of 2 Timothy, Paul answers that question with a deeply moving message: Remember your heritage.

As Paul seeks to forge in Timothy a "finish-line faith," he points the discouraged disciple backwards. Three times in 1:3-5, he speaks of remembering. Specifically, he stirs in Timothy the remembrance of his heritage.

Paul begins by mentioning his own heritage: "I serve as my forefathers did" (1:3). He then goes on to mention Timothy's heritage: "I have been reminded of your sincere faith, which first lived in your grandmother Lois and in your mother Eunice and, I am persuaded, now lives in you also."

I heard of a little girl who hesitantly approached her mother, "Mommy, do you remember the blue vase in the living room?" The mother asked, "Do you mean the one that's been passed down in my family from generation to generation?" The little girl sheepishly answered, "Yes, and this generation just dropped it."

Paul's message here is, "Timothy, don't be the generation that drops the faith. I am following in the footsteps of faith left by those who've gone before me. Now you follow in the footsteps left by those who've gone before you."

Surely these names in verse 5 evoked powerful memories for the thirty-something Timothy of his childhood years. We know that Timothy's father was a Greek, not a believer, but his grandmother and mother were Jewish. Very likely Lois, Eunice, and Timothy all became Christians under Paul's preaching in Lystra on his first missionary journey. (Acts 14:6-7) However, even before placing their faith in Christ, these two godly women taught the boy Timothy their Jewish Scriptures, what we call the Old Testament. In 2 Timothy 3:15, Paul says, "From infancy you have known the holy Scriptures." As the old reformer John Calvin put it, Timothy "was reared in his infancy in such a way that he could suck in godliness along with his mother's milk."[1]

> Paul's message is, "Don't be the generation that drops the faith."

What images flooded Timothy's memory here? Did he remember seeing his grandmother praying on her knees every morning as the sun rose? Did he think back to the times when his little heart pounded as his mother told bedtime stories of the Hebrew heroes of faith—Abraham, Joseph, Moses, David?

One thing is clear: Paul wants Timothy to find resolve in remembering. He wants Timothy to feel a strong sense of stewardship—a responsibility to preserve the godly heritage he has received. His grandmother and mother had remained faithful; he can do no less. Paul wants Timothy to feel it deep in his DNA: he has a tradition to keep. He must keep the faith alive. He can't quit the race because he has a baton to carry, a story to continue, an honor to uphold.

The leadership of each generation is the legacy they leave to the next.

When you feel discouraged and your pace is slowing, a backward look may help inspire forward motion. Recalling the stories of those who've gone before you can:

- *provide wisdom*. Their lives may show you what your guiding values look like when they're fleshed out. Their decisions can help shape yours.

*Remember Your Heritage*

- *deepen your sense of identity*. Only when you know who you came from can you know who you are. Even windshields come with rearview mirrors.
- *give you hope*. When you remember others who've persevered through trials to come out stronger, you begin to believe your own difficulties may not be fatal after all.
- *inspire faithfulness*. Their lives were in some way an investment in yours. Who would want to waste such a precious gift? Instead, you'll want your life to provide a healthy return on their investment.

## Your Biblical Heritage

But what exactly are the remembrances that firm up a faltering faith? What kind of heritage are we to remember? One type of heritage Paul references here is biblical. The apostle saw himself standing in the long line of his Old Testament "forefathers," following God the way Noah and Joshua and Daniel had centuries before. From this he drew strength.

The writer of Hebrews lived with similar wisdom. Writing to Jewish Christians who were considering discarding their faith in Jesus, in Hebrews 11 the author points them back to their great biblical heritage.

The movie *Rudy* is the true story of Daniel "Rudy" Ruettiger, who grew up dreaming of playing football for Notre Dame. Everyone tells him it's impossible, but his heart and hard work eventually get him into Notre Dame, where he makes the football team as a walk-on, plays for two downs in the last game of his senior year and officially enters the annals of Notre Dame football.

Halfway through the movie, he enters the Notre Dame locker room for the first time, and for Rudy, this is holy ground. He begins to move slowly through the darkened room, locker to locker, and in hushed tones, he begins to name Notre Dame's football history. "The Four Horsemen. Knute Rockne. Moose Krause. Angelo Bertelli. Johnny Lujack." He stops at a locker in awe, "Paul Hornung could've dressed in this locker."

When the going got tough for Daniel Ruettiger, it was that rich heritage that kept him going. He knew the story of Notre Dame football, and he wanted to be a small part of that great story.

Back to Hebrews 11, the author takes his readers through the darkened locker room of faith. As he moves from locker to locker, he tells in hushed tones the amazing stories of those who, against all odds, kept on trusting God. Their lives preach an unforgettable sermon. Each one "still speaks, even though he is dead" (Heb 11:4). It is their message of faithful endurance, echoing down through the years, that the Hebrews writer wants his readers to hear. He follows Hebrews 11 with this charge: "Therefore, since we are surrounded

The names in Hebrews 11 are your spiritual genealogy.

by such a great cloud of witnesses . . . let us run with perseverance the race marked out for us" (Heb 12:1).

That message is for you. That "great cloud of witnesses"—those are *your* spiritual ancestors. As a Christian, you are an heir of Abraham. As the Church, you are the new Israel. Those names in Hebrews 11 are your spiritual genealogy, and their faith courses through your veins. Their story is now your story, which means you can't quit. You're called to write the next chapter.

When you feel like giving up, reflect on your biblical heritage. "For everything that was written in the past was written to teach us, so that through endurance and the encouragement of the Scriptures we might have hope" (Rom 15:4). Find a character from Scripture that resonates with you, and meditate on his or her life. Of course, the greatest example in Scripture is Christ. "Let us fix our eyes on Jesus, the author and perfecter of our faith, who for the joy set before him endured the cross, scorning its shame, and sat down at the right hand of the throne of God. Consider him who endured such opposition from sinful men, so that you will not grow weary and lose heart" (Heb 12:2-3).

## Your Historical Heritage

Beyond the last page of Scripture, you will also find strength in the pages of church history, the stories of great saints through the ages. Perhaps you've never read the story of the aged Polycarp, a second-century martyr, who was given one last chance to recant his faith before being burned at the stake. His reply: "Eighty and six years have I served him, and he never once wronged me; how then can I blaspheme my King who saved me?"

Or the story of William Tyndale, who labored tirelessly to put into people's hands a Bible they could read in their own language. He eventually printed the first English New Testament, despite the Catholic Church's threats to execute anyone owning a non-Latin Bible. After suffering shipwreck, loss of manuscripts, exile, pursuit by secret agents, and betrayal by a friend, he was captured, strangled, and his dead body burned at the stake. (How can I ever take lightly this English Bible I hold in my hand?)

The great men and women of God down through history—Amy Carmichael, David Brainerd, Susanna Wesley, Jim Elliot, George Mueller—their lives move me. They remind me that I am not an island. I am part of a vast continent called the kingdom of God, and it stretches back through the centuries and around the globe. Church history did not start when I took my first ministry. I am part of a bigger story, and those who have walked before me inspire me.

Listen to my friend J.K. Jones tell his own story:

Church history did not start when I took my first ministry. I am part of a bigger story.

There was a season in the whirlwind of books, seminary and ministry where I believed I could not go on. Criticism, overwork and little rest took its toll. One Sunday night, after evening worship and a difficult meeting, I thought I was coming apart. I wondered if this was what it was like when a person had a "breakdown." I cried and couldn't stop. My wife took me and our family over to the home of dear friends. . . . Those precious people reached into their pockets and gave us all the cash they had . . . and offered these wise words, "Get out of the area code and let us know where you are." We loaded the car and drove all night, spending the next couple of weeks in Arkansas with my wife's parents.

I didn't think I wanted to go back to that ministry or to that church. My soul was dry, my mind dull, and my heart broken. My mother-in-law knew better than I did what was happening and what was at stake. For several days I said very little and mostly slept. One morning I heard a knock at the door of the bedroom. I didn't answer. The door creaked open, and Mom Graham threw me a Snickers candy bar and a book. The only word from her mouth was, "Enjoy."

I did not open either gift for a while, but slowly I began to eat the candy bar and then turned my appetite to the book. Mom had found an old copy of *The Biography of David Livingstone*.[2] I devoured it, reading and rereading words, sentences and paragraphs. Livingstone's life of courage, endurance and character spoke deeply to my soul. It was as if God himself spoke loudly and firmly through that book, "If Livingstone can persevere, so can you." After some more days of rest we returned, and our most productive years of ministry in that church followed.[3]

May I challenge you to read the lives of faithful Christians through the ages? Someone said, "Theology must always become biography," and when I see the truth of God fleshed out in the lives of people, it challenges me to do likewise.

## Your Personal Heritage

Not only can the history of the Church spur you to go the distance, so can the history of your particular congregation. The group of believers with whom you worship has a history as well. Do you know that story? Search the "institutional memory" of your congregation. Talk to the older members of the church; ask them questions about the good times and hard times in days gone by.

If you yourself are one of the "grayheads," be intentional about telling those stories—not to compare or complain, but to capture the characteristics that define your congregation. Like tribal elders, seize the moments "around the campfire" to pass on the oral history of your

Search the "institutional memory" of your congregation.

people to the young warriors. These stories can embed your congregation's historic commitment to excellence—or evangelistic heart, or sacrificial generosity, or risky faith—deep in the next generation's imagination.

In addition to your church family, your biological family may have given you a spiritual legacy. I heard about a mother explaining proudly to her daughter that her grandfather was a preacher, her great-great-grandfather was a preacher, and her great-great-great-grandfather was a preacher. The little girl replied, "Wow! We sure come from a long line of grandfathers."

Maybe you come from a long line of believers. It's been said that God has children, but no grandchildren, and it's true that no one gets into the

kingdom on the coattails of his parents. You can't inherit your family's faith; however you *can* certainly catch it. An authentic Christian example is contagious, and perhaps it was the witness of your mother or father, aunt or grandfather that brought you to Christ.

Maybe you did not have a Christian family, but you had a spiritual mentor of some kind. Someone told you and taught you about Jesus. While Timothy had a believing grandmother and mother, it was a mentor, Paul, who really discipled him in Christ. Notice how Paul highlights their personal relationship in our 2 Timothy text. He writes, "Recalling your tears, I long to see you, so that I may be filled with joy" (1:4). The apostle is reminding Timothy of his love for this discouraged young minister and of his past investment in Timothy's life (1:6). Perhaps you have a "Paul" who has poured into your life.

The point here is: think about your own personal heritage. When I'm having a hard day in ministry, I look up at the signatures on the "Certificate of Ordination" that hangs on my wall, the men who laid hands on me to set me apart for ministry:

- My dad—a corporate executive, elder, and the most servant-hearted man I know.
- My longtime hometown preacher—who recruited me to ministry and closed his sermons for thirty years with the words, "Remember: God loves you, Jesus loves you, and I love you." Somehow I knew he meant it.
- My father-in-law—a big, quiet farmer and church elder who passed away during the writing of this book. The line of people at his visitation lasted almost four hours. Generous and faithful, his life cast a long shadow.
- My grandfather—another elder and farmer. (Ironically his last name was Weede!) He only finished eighth grade, but for years, he was a diligent Bible student and teacher. He too went to be with the Lord during the writing of this book. He literally prayed for me by name every day from the day I was born until the day he died.

When I see those names, I realize: I can't quit.

Who's on your list of names? Someone invested in you. Whose faith "now lives in you" (1:5)? I have a student who keeps in the back of his Bible the pictures of those whose lives pointed him to God: a parent, a 19th-century missionary, a minister. Whose pictures would be in the back of your Bible?

When you're tired and feel like giving in, hear Paul's message to Timothy: remember your heritage and keep going on. A backward look can inspire forward motion.

By the way, don't forget: *your* example can shape those who come after you. If with God's help you finish well, your picture may someday be in the back of someone else's Bible.

The leadership of your generation is the legacy you'll leave to the next.

---

[1] Stott, *Message of 2 Timothy*, 27.

[2] You may remember that David Livingstone was the 19th-century Scottish missionary, doctor, and explorer who helped open central Africa to missions.

[3] J.K. Jones, *Reading with God in Mind* (Joplin, MO: Heartspring, 2003) 60-61.

# Going On When We Feel Like Giving In

1. What is your family's spiritual heritage? Did you grow up in a Christian family? Describe your background.

2. Name a character in the Bible that you identify with. Why? What lessons have you learned from that character's life?

3. Have you read much about Christian heroes through the ages—men and women from church history? What would be the value in learning more? Who could be a help in knowing where to start?

4. Who would be able to tell the stories of your congregation's heritage? Do you know any of those stories?

5. If you put together a list of those who invested in you, what names would it include? How have they invested in you? Whose list might you be on someday?

6. Write a note of thanks to someone on your list. If they have already passed away, write a prayer of thanks to God for these people.

**Memory Verse**
2 Tim 1:5

*I have been reminded of your sincere faith, which first lived in your grandmother Lois and in your mother Eunice and, I am persuaded, now lives in you also.*

❖

C
H
A
P
T
E
R

2 *Remember Your Heritage*

# CHAPTER THREE

# RELY ON THE SPIRIT

### 2 TIMOTHY 1:6-7

*"Christian sermons ought to ask more of people than mortals can rightfully do . . . because we are equipped with inward supernatural potency, thanks to the Holy Spirit. Christians have in the Holy Spirit more power than they know what to do with."*

—*Lee Eclov*

Growing up, I dreamed of being Superman.

That's because as a child I was profoundly unheroic. I was skinny—a whopping 135 pounds at high school graduation—with pencil-thin arms and a paper-thin chest. I had little athletic ability, wore glasses, and preferred reading books to meeting people. I was such a bookworm that, when I disobeyed my parents, they grounded me for a week . . . *from reading!* Can you get any nerdier than that? I felt like an eight-year-old Clark Kent—awkward, fumbling, and powerless.

That's why, when the movie *Superman* swooped into theaters, my imagination was captured. When I saw the Man of Steel soaring through the sky, I wanted to fly! If only I too could deflect bullets and sprint faster than a speeding locomotive. To have supernatural power coursing through my body, the abilities to manage any mayhem that life might throw my way—that's what I longed for.

I'm not the only boy who's had this dream. Writing of his childhood, John Ortberg says, "I wanted to be Superman. I wanted his X-ray vision, wanted to bend steel with my bare hands, and most of all wanted his chest, with that giant red S on it. I never had the kind of chest that could accommodate a red S—a less curvy letter, perhaps, a lowercase *l* or *i*."[1] I could identify.

So could Timothy. I don't know if he had a skinny chest, but Timothy did have a weak stomach, hesitant voice, and faint heart. He feels like Clark Kent without the alter-ego. Staring into the teeth of a challenging church, he feels powerless. The bad guys in Ephesus are not imaginary. (see 2 Tim 3:1-9.) They are potent adversaries, and Timothy knows he's no hero. Where will he ever find the strength to deal with these difficulties?

Ever asked that question? Maybe you're facing a formidable foe—cancer, conflict, a dark temptation—and wondering how you will handle it. You are painfully aware of your own limitations, and as you size up the situation, you know your resources—physical, emotional, intellectual—are simply not enough.

Where can a guy find superpowers when he really needs them?

In 2 Timothy 1:6-7, Paul gives the answer: the Holy Spirit.

## Who Is the Holy Spirit?

Before going further, we need to set a theological context for these two verses, because the Holy Spirit can be a mysterious figure. You may recognize His picture in the Bible when you see it—a wind, a fire, a dove—but you may not know much about Him. Dorothy Sayers told of a Japanese believer, new to the faith, who was struggling to understand Christian teaching. "Honorable Father, very good," he said to his missionary teacher. "Honorable Son, very good. But Honorable Bird, I do not understand at all."[2] Briefly, what does the Bible teach about the Holy Spirit?

First, the Holy Spirit is *a personal being*. Some mistakenly picture Him as simply an impersonal force. As one misguided teacher put it, "The Holy Spirit is not a person, but the power God the Father uses—much as a man uses electricity."[3] Rather, He is a person with consciousness, personality, and a will (Acts 13:2; 15:28). In fact, in places like John 16:13-14, the masculine personal pronoun "he" is used in reference to the Spirit. After my recent trip to the barber, I do not want my students to say, "Oh, look, *it* got a new haircut." I am not a thing, but a person, and so is the Holy Spirit. Call Him "He."

Second, the Holy Spirit is *a divine being*. Unfortunately, He is sometimes treated like the junior member of the Trinity, the kid brother of the Godhead. If the Trinity was a church staff, then the Holy Spirit would be the youth pastor—no respect. However, the Bible teaches His full equality with the Father and Son, divine in every sense they are. He is eternal (Heb 9:14), omnipresent (Ps 139:7-10), knows everything God knows (1 Cor 2:10-11), and helped create the world (Gen 1:2, Ps 104:30). In Matthew 28:19, the disciples are commanded to baptize "in the name of the Father and the Son and the Holy Spirit," clearly placing the Spirit at the same level as the first and second Persons of the Trinity.

Third, for the believer, the Holy Spirit is *an indwelling being*. I heard a preacher say once that the Father is God *without* skin, Jesus is God *with* skin, and the Holy Spirit is God *within my* skin. When we are baptized by faith into Christ, the Spirit comes to live within us (Acts 2:38). The Holy Ghost becomes our Holy Guest. In the Old Testament, God promised to be *with* His people, but in the New Testament, God promises to be *in* His people. What a difference a preposition makes! As a Christian, I am called to imitate Christ, but on my own, I can no more live like Jesus than I can paint like Rembrandt or play basketball like Michael Jordan.

But what if the spirit of Rembrandt lived *inside* me, painting his portraits with my hands? What if Michael Jordan could somehow inhabit my body and play basketball through me? My performance (on the canvas or on the court) wouldn't be perfect, but it would be more than I could ever achieve on my own. Likewise, while I can't imitate Christ in my own strength, His Spirit in me can live His life through me. I'll never look exactly like Him, but I'll be much closer because He's not just with me, but *in* me.

It's this transforming truth that Paul emphasizes for Timothy. Look at 2 Timothy 1:6, 1:7, 1:8, 1:14, and 2:2. In each verse, he references God's power that is available to us—no, *in* us. The message is clear: You may feel like Clark Kent, but through the Holy Spirit, supernatural abilities can be yours.

## The Spirit Gives Supernatural Ability to Serve

In 2 Timothy 1:6, Paul challenges Timothy to "fan into flame the gift of God, which is in you through the laying on of my hands." Paul seems to be reminding Timothy of his "ordination service," when a group of elders and the apostle himself laid hands on him, spoke words of exhortation, and imparted a spiritual gift to him (1 Tim 4:14). This is one way the Holy Spirit empowers the believer: the endowment of spiritual gifts.

A spiritual gift is *a supernatural ability that equips a believer for service to God's people.* In some cases, the Spirit simply supernaturally enhances a natural ability someone already has and directs it toward kingdom use. (Of course, the natural ability was originally from God as well.) A capable leader in the business world, upon coming to Christ, may become a gifted leader in the church.

In other cases, the ability is completely new to the believer. A high school speech teacher once told my friend Stacy that his class presentation was so bad that he should never speak in public again. (This teacher clearly did not have the gift of encouragement.) But when he became a Christian at age 19, Stacy believed God had called him to preach and, thanks to the Spirit's gifting, became a very effective proclaimer of God's Word.

If we were to download the major New Testament texts on spiritual gifts (1 Cor 12:1-31; Rom 12:4-8; Eph 4:7-16; 1 Pet 4:10-11), at least two truths would stand out:

- *Every believer has a gift.* Some may think, "When God was handing out gifts, He must've missed me." But last time I checked, God doesn't make spare people. He doesn't keep extra human beings around that He's not planning to use. While some may have a  greater number of gifts (like the 5 talent servant in Matt 25:14-30), everybody has at least one ability to use in service. (See 1 Cor 12:7; 12:11; and 1 Pet 4:10.) If you have the Spirit, you have a spiritual gift.

- *Spiritual gifts come in all shapes and sizes.* When speaking of gifts, we can often focus on one or two that are prominent, like preaching or leadership. But even a quick read through the above passages will show: *many* Spirit-given abilities are necessary for building up the church—mercy, encouragement, giving, and more. A gift that is more "behind-the-scenes" is no less important than those which are "up front."

We don't exactly know what gift the Spirit had bestowed on Timothy, but whatever it was, Timothy apparently considered shelving it. In 1 Timothy 4:14, Paul says, "Do not neglect your gift," or as *The Message* translates it, "That special gift of ministry you were given . . . keep that dusted off and in use." Again in 2 Timothy 1:6, Paul is urging this young pastor to keep his gift warmed up and ready to go. The Spirit had empowered him for ministry, and to keep that ministry gift under wraps would be like Superman refusing to use his powers to help other people.

May I do some "urging" with you for a moment? Spiritual gifts are wonderful grace-presents from God to the church, but they carry with them a few inherent dangers.

*Don't use them as a cop-out for radical service.* When the toilet is overflowing in the church bathroom, don't walk by with the "sorry-I-can't-help-because-my-gift-is-evangelism" excuse. Grab a plunger. We're all called to serve, even if it's not always in our giftedness "sweet spot."

*Don't use them as a substitute for spiritual maturity.* The gifts of the Spirit cannot take the place of the fruit of the Spirit (Gal 5:22-23). I've met a few Christians who acted like their special gifts—preaching, music, whatever—exempted them from virtues like humility and patience. Read Paul's first letter to the gifted-but-immature church in Corinth: a certain kind of competence does not make Christlike character optional.

*Don't misuse them out of pride.* We might be tempted to use our abilities to gain personal recognition, but spiritual gifts are for the building of God's kingdom, not our own. First Peter 4:10 says they are to be used "to serve others," and 1 Corinthians 12:7 says gifts are "given for the common good."

*Don't "unuse" them out of laziness or fear.* The church needs all hands on deck. "Practice of the biblical doctrine of gifts taps reservoirs of godly man-power, thaws out frozen assets, roots out unemployment among saints, reflects the universal priesthood of believers and edifies the church."[4] So discover your gifts by examining your life, trying different kinds of service opportunities and asking for others' input on what you do best. Once you find your spiritual strong suit, make the most of it. Christianity is not a spectator sport. As a friend of mine says, "You got into the ministry when you got out of the baptistery." Use your gift.

## The Spirit Gives Supernatural Ability to Endure

Not only does the Holy Spirit give the ability to serve, but also the ability to endure. He is the one who forges in us a "finish-line faith." No matter what you face, says Paul, the indwelling presence of God is enough to sustain you. As one church sign read, "The problem before us is never as great as the power within us."

> The Holy Spirit gives both the ability to serve and the ability to endure.

And make no mistake: there certainly will be problems. In verse 7, Paul says, "For God did not give us a spirit of timidity, but a spirit of power, of love and of self-discipline." The word "timidity" was sometimes used in ancient times of "cowardice in battle," and Timothy will fight battles on many fronts. Manipulative false teachers, wayward church members, lone-liness, physical fatigue, the temptations that usually plague a young single man in a sexually charged culture—all of these will war against his soul. But Paul reminds Timothy of the spiritual resources the Holy Spirit will provide. Specifically, he mentions three.

### Power to Endure Difficult Circumstances

The first Spirit-resource Paul mentions in 2 Timothy 1:7 is "power." The Greek word here is *dunamis*, from which we form our English word "dynamite." Paul's constant prayer for God's people was that "out of his glorious riches he may strengthen you with power through his Spirit in your inner being" (Eph 3:16). William Barclay said this *dunamis* is "the power to shoulder the back-breaking task, the power to stand erect in face of the shattering situation, the power to retain faith in face of the soul-searing sorrow and the wounding disappointment."[5]

I heard a preacher once tell the story of a float in the Rose Bowl parade which suddenly came to a stop. It had run out of gas, backing up the entire procession. The irony: the float represented the Standard Oil Company! They had failed to tap the vast reservoirs of fuel at their disposal. Too often we as Christians try to tackle life's challenges in our strength, without tap-ping the vast and available power of God. As writer Andree Seu confesses,

"I've whined so much about a poor memory, depression, and insomnia that a friend suggested I take a bottle of 'white out' and delete Philippians 4:13 since I wasn't using it anyway."

How do we access the Spirit's power? Quite simply, by faith. Will you really trust God to do "immeasurably more than all we ask or imagine, according to his power that is at work within us" (Eph 3:20)? Will you refuse to see as hyperbole, "Everything is possible for him who believes" (Mark 9:23)? Will you actually expect to be "strengthened with all power according to his glorious might so that you may have great endurance and patience" (Col 1:11)? For those believers who will, they will "look at the size of their problems and then look at the size of Resurrection power and decide there's no contest."[6]

Richard Wurmbrand experienced that power. Wurmbrand was the founder of the *Voice of the Martyrs* ministry. As a pastor in Romania behind the Iron Curtain he was arrested in 1948 and tortured for 14 years because of his faith in Christ. In his book *Tortured for Christ*, he wrote, "It was strictly forbidden to preach to other prisoners. . . . It was understood that whoever was caught doing this received a severe beating. But a number of us decided to pay the price for the privilege of preaching, so we accepted their terms. It was a deal: we preached and they beat us. We were happy preaching; they were happy beating us—so everyone was happy."

Listen: That kind of power is simply not natural. Normal people do not endure circumstances that difficult and call themselves "happy." Your average Clark Kent couldn't take that. That must be a power from somewhere outside this world, a power from heaven. Mind you, this supernat-

ural power that courses through our veins doesn't mean we are free from pain. Bullets didn't bounce off Jesus' chest. When life wounds us, we will still bleed. But this supernatural Spirit power does mean we can come through these crises to finish strong.

## Love to Endure Difficult People

The second Spirit-resource Paul lists in 1:7 is "love." The Greek word here is *agape*, which someone defined as "an unconditional commitment to an imperfect person." Timothy surely faced some imperfect people in Ephesus—folks with bad attitudes, immature thinking, unwise habits, and needy personalities.

Welcome to the church.

Every congregation has difficult people. Someone said, "If you want to be the light of the world, you're going to attract a few bugs." My hunch is that there are a few folks in your church that bug you. Or maybe they're outside the church—a boss, a neighbor, or a family member that frustrates you, perhaps even antagonizes you. At best, they drive you to impatience. At worst, they stir within you feelings of anger, bitterness, and even hatred.

How will we ever learn to *love* such people? Only by the Spirit's work in our lives. Love is first in the list of the fruit of the Spirit, remember, and as we listen to His promptings in our life, we will learn to seek the best for these difficult people. He will guide our actions toward them, and eventually our hearts will follow.

During my junior year in Bible college, I was convinced the two freshmen in the dorm room next to mine were not going to heaven. They stayed up late, slept through classes, played their rock music loudly, and proudly displayed their support for the Los Angeles Lakers.

Clearly, they were pagans.

One night, as I was studying, they turned their music up, and I reached my breaking point. I stormed next door and vented my righteous indignation. Someone said that, when you're angry, you'll give the best speech you'll ever regret, and that night I gave those guys a really good speech.

When I returned to my room to resume studying, I calmed down, and as I did, I could hear the Holy Spirit's convicting whisper: "Go apologize." I did not *want* to go apologize, so for the next hour, I wrestled with the Holy Spirit. "They deserved it," I argued. "They need someone to offer correction. I need to study. I've been patient for several weeks." But the Spirit deflected every rationalizing move I made and pinned me to the mat with two realizations: I had harbored a judgmental spirit, and I had spoken inexcusable, harsh words.

So I went back later that evening and apologized. In the weeks afterward, a strange thing began to happen. Every time I passed their room, instead of rehearsing their past offenses, I began to pray for them. The Spirit slowly began to melt the coldness I'd allowed to overtake my heart, and I grew to appreciate those two guys. Today they both have fruitful ministries, and I'm privileged to call them friends. But I couldn't manufacture that love on my own. Only the Spirit within me could make that happen.

### Self-Discipline to Endure Difficult Temptations

The last Spirit-resource Paul mentions is "self-discipline." The Greek word used here means "control of yourself in the face of passion." Whether the temptation is greed, lust, anger, or pride, the Spirit helps the believer overcome the passions that war against us.

How does the Spirit do this? The word "self-discipline" has within it the idea of "good judgment, wise thinking." The devil is a master deceiver, whispering lies to distort our thinking. He knows that, when we believe a false reality, we will behave in self-destructive ways. In this spiritual battle, the Spirit counters by whispering truth, helping us to see life as it really is. When we perceive true reality, we can behave in self-disciplined ways.

Not only does the Spirit give us the *truth* that we need to rightly evaluate tempting moments. He also gives us the supernatural *discipline* we need to rightly act in those moments. Left to my own strength, I will too often choose the wrong, even when I know it's wrong (read Rom 7:14-25). In the face of temptation, I am profoundly unheroic. I am that skinny, fumbling, powerless eight-year-old Clark Kent all over again. That's why the Spirit's power is the only thing that will keep me "going on when I feel like giving in."

No matter what foe you are facing—challenging circumstances, frustrating people, dark temptations—the Holy Spirit of God within you can transform you in heroic ways. When you emerge from God's telephone booth, you can stand tall with a big red "S" on your chest. That "S" doesn't stand for Superman, but it does stand for "Spirit-filled." In the Holy Spirit, you have supernatural power! As we rely on Him, we can finish strong.

[1] John Ortberg, *The Life You've Always Wanted* (Grand Rapids: Zondervan, 1997) 107.
[2] Robertson McQuilken, *Life in the Spirit* (Nashville: Broadman and Holman, 2000) ix.
[3] Cited in Jack Cottrell, *The Holy Spirit: A Biblical Study* (Joplin, MO: College Press, 2006) 8.
[4] Leslie Flynn, *19 Gifts of the Spirit* (Wheaton, IL: Victor, 1994) 16.
[5] William Barclay, *The Letters to Timothy, Titus and Philemon*, Daily Study Bible (Louisville, KY: Westminster John Knox, 1975) 144.
[6] Andree Seu, "The Power of Now," *World* magazine 20 (Oct. 29, 2005).

# Going On When We Feel Like Giving In

1. If you could have any superpower, what would it be?

2. How comfortable are you talking about the Holy Spirit? Do you have any uneasiness? Do you feel like you're aware of His presence in your life? How?

3. Describe what you think your spiritual gifts might be. Would you say you are using them, misusing them, or not using them? What might be a way to use your gifts within the next two weeks to help the church?

4. What difficult circumstances are you currently facing that you need Holy-Spirit power to endure?

5. Do you have difficult people in your life? If the Holy Spirit gave you the ability to love them, what would that look like, practically speaking?

6. Name a temptation that you need the Holy Spirit's supernatural power to overcome. Ask God to give you the Spirit-resources you need this week to overcome.

*For God did not give us a spirit of timidity, but a spirit of power, of love and of self-discipline.*

# CHAPTER FOUR

# MEDITATE ON THE GOSPEL

## 2 TIMOTHY 1:8-12

*"Men more frequently require to be reminded than informed."*
—Samuel Johnson

Psychologists study a phenomenon called "habituation." When a new stimulus is introduced into your environment, you are at first intensely aware of it. But over time this awareness begins to fade, and you "habituate." For example, when you begin to wear a new wristwatch, you can feel it on your arm the first day or two. But within a few days, your nervous system "ignores" the weight of the watch, and you don't even know it's there. You have habituated.

Sometimes, out of long habit, we can ignore experiences that once sparked our amazement. On a trip to Yellowstone National Park, author Philip Yancey ate at a restaurant with large windows facing Old Faithful. When the famous geyser erupted, he noticed the patrons were drawn in wonder to the sight, but the servers continued their duties without even a glance toward the windows. It no longer captured their attention. They felt no awe. After long familiarity, they had habituated.

### Spiritual Habituation

You have probably sung John Newton's hymn *Amazing Grace* many times, but here's my question: are you still amazed by the gospel? Or have you habituated?

A few years ago, I accompanied our church's elementary kids to a local production of the Passion Play. The group included several un-churched kids from a pretty rough neighborhood—street kids. I don't want to call them obnoxious, but let's just say that sitting politely for an hour in an auditorium waiting for the production to begin was not their spiritual gift. It was a Friday night. I was tired. I was riding herd on a third-grader named David who kept harassing the other kids, being disruptive, and telling dirty jokes. To be honest, I was ready for the evening to be over before the play even started.

Finally the lights went down, and to my surprise, within moments David was captivated, eyes wide with wonder. He had never heard the story of Jesus, so as the play unfolded, he kept asking me questions in the dark. Slowly I began to see the familiar story through David's fresh eyes.

When Jesus came down the aisle bearing His cross, within inches of where we sat, David was transfixed. The soldiers began pounding the nails, and David turned to me in genuine grief and asked, "Why are the soldiers doing that? Why are they killing Him?"

I tried to explain simply, "Jesus hadn't done anything wrong. He let the soldiers kill Him to take the punishment for our sins. Those other two men on the crosses were criminals. They died for the bad things they did. But Jesus died for the bad things *we* did."

David said, with tears in his eyes, "That's not fair!"

I gave the only reply I could, "You're right, David. It wasn't fair. But He did it because He loved us."

I offered him a Kleenex, and suddenly it hit me: it had been a long time since my heart was broken by the cross. When was the last time I wept at the foot of Calvary? I'd heard the story so many times that I guess I'd gotten used to it. Like the servers at the Old Faithful restaurant, long familiarity had drained out my sense of wonder.

> Sometimes the greatest danger I face is not spiritual rebellion. It's spiritual habituation.

Sometimes the greatest danger I face is not spiritual rebellion. It's spiritual habituation.

## Remembering Our Blessings

Samuel Johnson once said we don't need to be informed of new truths as much as reminded of old truths. So in 2 Timothy 1:8, Paul reminds Timothy of the gospel he has experienced. Paul knows that when we spiritually "habituate," we no longer feel a sense of amazed thankfulness; we can take the gift of salvation for granted. Our motivation for persevering grows weak. We maximize our chances of finishing poorly when we minimize "such a great salvation" (Heb 2:3).

But as Timothy meditates again on the gospel, Paul hopes Timothy will be moved to gratitude. Psychological studies show that grateful people are more enthusiastic, more determined and stronger.[1] Remembering our blessings can actually renew our spirits. When we are once again amazed

*Meditate on the Gospel*

at God's love for us, we will once again be resolved to live fully for Him. Counting our blessings motivates us to make our blessings count.

So as he challenges Timothy to suffer for the gospel, Paul reminds him of the gospel's content. What does this incredible gift from God include? In 2 Timothy 1:8-12, Paul lists at least three blessings.

## Grace for Our Past

In verse 9, Paul points to God's grace as the *basis* for our salvation. God has chosen us to be forgiven, washed clean, adopted as His children and the objects of His love. Is this because we are worthy—such wonderful people that of course He would want us? The answer is emphatically NO. This word "grace" is often defined as *"unmerited* favor."

No one is moral enough, nice enough, gifted enough to warrant God's attention or earn His salvation. We offer absolutely NOTHING. As William Temple said, "The only thing of my very own which I contribute to redemption is the sin from which I need to be redeemed."

That's the ugly fact: we are sinners (Rom 3:23). We all have chosen to disobey God (Read through the Ten Commandments sometime and count how many you have never broken. You'll be dismayed.) We are rebels, and the punishment we deserve for our sin is death (Rom 6:23).

### Grace vs. Karma

But it is exactly at this point that God's grace enters. We all know the law of the universe is that you reap what you sow. It's what some call *karma*: if you do bad stuff, then bad stuff eventually comes back to you. Because we have sinned, the natural result would be punishment. But grace is the opposite of karma. In an illogical, unreasonable, surprising twist, God decides to interrupt the consequences of our actions. Instead of punishment, He offers forgiveness. Instead of wrath, He pours out love . . . all at the cost of His own Son (1:9).

*We are not an accident or an afterthought. God planned Calvary before He prepared Creation.*

Don't miss an important fact: God made the decision to give us this astonishing grace "before the beginning of time" (1:9). Sometimes I cringe when I hear parents refer to an unexpected child as our "oops" baby, as if she were an accident. But our arrival in God's family was not unplanned. We are not an accident or an afterthought. God wanted us so much that He planned Calvary before He prepared Creation.

That is nothing short of incredible. Inexplicably, God decided from eternity past to trade the life of His perfect Son for a bunch of imperfect wretches. My third-grade friend David was right: that trade is not fair. But God made it with forethought, and He made it because He loves us.

Even the fact that God "called us to a holy life" is an act of grace (1:9). It means that God is calling us to be His, to be a part of His family, to take on the habits of His family—which happen to be holy habits. God wants us to be His.

## Do vs. Done

Mary Ann Bird once experienced such grace. In her book *The Whisper Test*, she writes:

> I grew up knowing I was different, and I hated it. I was born with a cleft palate, and when I started school, my classmates made it clear to me how I looked to others: a little girl with a misshapen lip, crooked nose, lopsided teeth, and garbled speech.
>
> When classmates asked, "What happened to your lip?" I'd tell them I'd fallen and cut it on a piece of glass. Somehow it seemed more acceptable to have suffered an accident than to have been born different. I was convinced that no one outside my family could love me.
>
> There was, however, a teacher in the second grade whom we all adored—Mrs. Leonard by name. She was short, round, happy—a sparkling lady.
>
> Annually we had a hearing test. . . . Mrs. Leonard gave the test to everyone in the class, and finally it was my turn. I knew from past years that as we stood against the door and covered one ear, the teacher sitting at her desk would whisper something, and we would have to repeat it back—things like "The sky is blue" or "Do you have new shoes?" I waited there for those words that God must have put into her mouth, those seven words that changed my life. Mrs. Leonard said, in her whisper, "I wish you were my little girl."[2]

This is grace. Despite the fact that we are deeply marred by sin, God chooses us to be His children. He whispers, "I want you to be Mine." Such a move is startling, unforeseen. Grace is the great reversal, and because it comes so unexpectedly, so undeserved, grace is the "turn" in the story that catches our breath. Our hearts are stunned. Who ever could have guessed we were loved like *that*?

It turns out that the gospel is not, as the world assumes, a list of don'ts and dos. It is spelled D-O-N-E! The gospel is not about earning God's love; it is the joyous announcement that God already loves us. It is the good news that, in Jesus, He has already forgiven our sins. Our past is no longer held against us. God's arms are thrown wide open to receive us, and all we have to do is walk into His embrace.

> Grace is the great reversal.

I can't prove it, but I'm betting that, as Timothy read these words, he felt new motivation surging in his soul, and he whispered one word as he shook his head: *Amazing.*

# Hope for Our Future

If the first blessing of salvation is grace for our past, the second blessing Paul lists is hope for our future.

Since Genesis 3, the future of humankind has been summed up in a single word: death. It is the destiny of us all. Statistics show that 1 out of every 1 human beings dies. No one escapes.

I read about a lady in Greenville, South Carolina, who received the following letter from the Department of Social Services, "Your food stamps will be stopped effective March 1992 because we received notice that you passed away. May God bless you. You may reapply if your circumstances change."

Sorry to be the bearer of bad news, but "circumstances" don't change. Once you move into the graveyard, you can't decide later to move out. No one escapes death. Death is, quite simply, our greatest enemy. The scoreboard of history reads, "Death: 100 billion; Humanity: 0."

## Christ's Resurrection

But then came Jesus. In 2 Timothy 1:10, Paul pictures Christ in hand-to-hand combat with Death. On Good Friday, the battle was joined, and at first it looked like Death had triumphed again. At the end of the day, Christ was dead—no pulse, lifeless, laying-there-rigid-on-the-stone-cold-table-in-the-tomb dead.

He lay there dead Friday night. He lay there dead Saturday morning. He lay there dead Saturday night.

But then came Sunday morning. As the first rays of dawn broke over the horizon, a voice came rumbling in on the wind—a whisper from God Himself pierced the walls of that garden tomb: "Arise, my Son."

As those words echoed deep inside that cave, something happened. A heart that was still as the grave . . . suddenly began to beat again. Blood thick and cold rushed warmly through the veins. A chest heaved upward, taking in a great breath. Stiff fingers moved, eyes opened, arms raised, legs swung off the table—He was standing again, life radiating from Him as heat from the sun—He was alive! Christ had risen!

The world had never seen anything like this before. All previous raisings in the Bible—the Shunammite's boy, the widow of Nain's son, Lazarus— were resuscitations more than resurrections. They each came back to life only to someday die again. Death eventually claimed them as his.

But the resurrection of Jesus Christ was not a momentary victory. It

was not a temporary reprieve. In verse 10, Paul says Christ "destroyed death." He had broken its power, and Death could never again claim Him. The scoreboard now read: "Death: 100 billion; Humanity 1."

## Our Resurrection

Even that score will someday change. The Bible is clear that Christ's resurrection was a preview of coming attractions (see 1 Cor 15:20-23). If we belong to Him, someday we too will be raised from the dead to "life and immortality" (1:10). We will live, never to die again.

And what a life it will be! The word "immortality" here actually means "incorruptibility." Now we live in a world corrupted by sin and death and time. Let's just think of the effects of time. With the passing days, cars rust, fruit rots, and our bodies break down and wear out. The second law of thermodynamics—the universe is running down—gets us all. Time is not our friend. My grandpa was a farmer and could work from sunup to sundown—a strong and strapping man in his day. But as the years went by, he moved more slowly. His hearing and eyesight dimmed, his back was weak. His body suffered the effects of a corrupted world.

But what if we lived in an incorruptible world? A comedian once imagined what life would look like if time worked backward:

> I think the life cycle is all backward. You should die first, get that out of the way. Then you live twenty years in an old-age home where you wake up feeling better each day. Then you get kicked out when you're too young. You go collect your pension and get a gold watch on your first day at work. You work forty years until you're young enough to enjoy your retirement. You go to college and have a great time with your friends until you're ready for high school. You go to grade school; you become a little kid; you play. You have no responsibilities. You become a little baby; you go back into the womb; you spend your last nine months floating peacefully, and you finish up as a gleam in somebody's eye.[3]

When we read that, we laugh. But what if? If there is time in eternity, what if it somehow works backwards? Every day is fresher and brighter than the one before. The second law of thermodynamics is suddenly reversed, and everything gets better with time. Fruit gets sweeter, clothes get newer, floors get cleaner. Every morning in the new heavens and new earth my grandpa will wake up to go work in the fields he loved, and he will feel stronger and healthier and younger than the day before. We will be raised to experience "immortality"—the incredible hope of a world uncorrupted by sin and death and even time itself (see 1 Cor 15:42).

So for the Christian, death is no longer the end of the road, but a bend in the road. It is no longer the period at the end of the sentence of life, but a comma—transitioning us from this life to the next. Jesus kicked the end out of the tomb and turned it into a tunnel to eternal life! We can see the light streaming through even now. Now we can exult with Paul,

Jesus kicked the end out of the tomb and turned it into a tunnel to eternal life.

*Meditate on the Gospel*

"Where, O death, is your victory? Where, O death, is your sting? . . . Thanks be to God! He gives us the victory through our Lord Jesus Christ."

That hope gives us the strength to persevere. The apostle Peter said that we have been given "a living hope through the resurrection of Jesus Christ from the dead and . . . in this you greatly rejoice, though now for a little while you may have had to suffer grief in all kinds of trials" (1 Pet 1:3-6). No matter the difficulties we face, we know how our story will end. If we finish, we win.

While I can't prove it, I'm betting that as Timothy meditated on this deep hope, he once again shook his head and whispered: *Amazing.*

## Power for the Present

Paul mentions one final blessing in the gift of salvation: power for our present. In verse 8, Paul tells Timothy that the power to endure his present suffering will come from God. On the heels of verse 7, Paul is likely referring to the power of the Holy Spirit, which we discussed in the last chapter. The indwelling Holy Spirit is part of God's gift of salvation, and it is the Spirit who gives believers the strength to live each day for God.

### The Power Paul Experienced

You'll notice that Paul concludes this paragraph of Scripture with his own example of empowered endurance. He describes his ministry with three words. He calls himself:

- A *herald*, which is "someone who makes announcements on behalf of the king." It's translated elsewhere as *preacher* (2 Pet 2:5). Paul's ministry included *proclaiming* the gospel.
- An *apostle* which is "someone chosen directly by Christ to speak with Christ's authority." Thus the Twelve, plus Paul, were the official keepers of sound doctrine. Paul's ministry included *guarding* the gospel.
- A *teacher* which is "someone who gives instruction on Christian doctrine and its ethical implications." The early church didn't have the New Testament yet, with its descriptions of a Christian life. So Paul's ministry included *explaining* the gospel.

As you can see, Paul had a lot to do in his ministry! Of course, he had to do all this heralding and "apostling" and teaching in the midst of hardships like imprisonment, shipwrecks, and stonings. How did Paul endure?

The simple answer: by trusting God to get him through. In verse 12, Paul says he is "convinced" that God is powerful enough to guard "what I have entrusted to him"—namely, Paul's life. The apostle is saying, "I put my life in God's hands, and God's hands are strong enough to take care of me." It is not Paul's strength that gets him through; it is God's. Paul had the track record to prove it.

- When Paul was shipwrecked, God's power rescued him.
- When Paul was stoned, God's power raised him back up.
- When Paul was imprisoned, God's power sustained him.
- When Paul was targeted by assassins, God's power protected him.
- When Paul was physically weak, God's power carried him.[4]

Paul wants Timothy to know: what God has done for me, He will do for you. He is saying, "Don't forget, Timothy. Remember again the Mighty Presence who makes Himself available to you. The same Holy Spirit that strengthens me will strengthen you. The same Father who has given me power to endure will also empower you."

*When we put our lives in God's hands, they are strong enough to take care of us.*

## The Power We Can Experience

In the 1992 Summer Olympics in Barcelona, Derek Redmond of Great Britain is a favorite for a medal in the 400 meter race. The runners line up, the gun sounds, and Derek quickly seizes the lead. But with 175 meters to go, Redmond suddenly pulls up and falls to the track, clutching his right leg. He has pulled his hamstring, the other runners have finished, and tears begin to stream down his face. It appears his Olympic dream is over.

Up in the stands, Derek's father Jim watches in disbelief. Immediately he begins racing down from the top row to the track, bumping some people and sidestepping others in his hurry. Later he told the press, "I wasn't going to be stopped by anyone."

Down on the track, Derek grimaces in pain, but he refuses the medical crew with the stretcher. Instead, in a moment that will live forever in my mind, Derek lifts himself to his feet and begins to hobble down the track, hopping on one leg. He is not limping to the side of the track to drop out. No, he is going to finish the race on one leg. He will cross the finish-line. The crowd stands to its feet and begins to cheer, then roar.

Derek hobbles on, each step slower than the last, his face twisted in pain. Then unexpectedly, another figure runs onto the track behind him. Jim Redmond has leaped over the railing, evaded the security personnel, and now he runs alongside Derek. The father puts his arm around the son, and the son collapses momentarily, sobbing into the father's shoulder. Then together, arm in arm—with 65,000 people clapping, cheering, and crying—father and son finish the race.

The Father gives us the strength to finish the race.

In the press and fury of our lives, we can forget. In our heads we intellectually know that God has already given us in the Holy Spirit the power we need, but in our day-to-day experience, we can forget. We habituate.

But Paul tells Timothy and tells us: don't forget. Meditate again on the incredible gift of salvation—grace for our past, hope for our future, and power for our present. We really can endure the hardships and cross the finish line . . . not in our own power, but in His.

While I can't prove it, I'm betting that as Timothy remembered again the power now at work within him, he shook his head and whispered one word: *Amazing.* 🔲

---

[1] Dr. Robert Emmons, "Pay It Forward," *Greater Good* (Summer 2007) 12-15

[2] Quoted in Les Parrott, *High-Maintenance Relationships* (Wheaton, IL: Tyndale House, 1997) 236.

[3] Quoted in Mike Yaconelli, *Dangerous Wonder* (Colorado Springs, CO: NavPress, 1998).

[4] See Acts 27:24; 14:19-20; 2 Tim 4:17; Acts 23:16; 2 Cor 12:9.

4   *Meditate on the Gospel*

# Going On When We Feel Like Giving In

1. Have you ever experienced spiritual "habituation"? What used to excite or amaze you that you have now grown too familiar with?

2. Go through the 10 commandments (Exod 20:3-17) and keep track of how many you have never broken. Without sharing it with the group, what was your score? How does this exercise make you feel?

3. Sometimes we spell Christianity D-O (a list of things we must do to earn God's favor) instead of D-O-N-E. Have you ever fallen into that way of thinking? How so?

4. How has death touched your life? How does the hope of resurrection change your thinking about death? What part of the hope of heaven excites you the most?

5. Give an instance when you have experienced God's power in your life.

6. Take time to thank God in amazement again for His great salvation.

**Memory Verse**
2 Tim 1:8b-10

*. . . join with me in suffering for the gospel, by the power of God, <sup>9</sup>who has saved us and called us to a holy life—not because of anything we have done but because of his own purpose and grace. This grace was given us in Christ Jesus before the beginning of time, <sup>10</sup>but it has now been revealed through the appearing of our Savior, Christ Jesus, who has destroyed death and has brought life and immortality to light through the gospel.*

45

✛

C
H
A
P
T
E
R

4

*Meditate on the Gospel*

CHAPTER FIVE

# GUARD THE TRUTH

## 2 TIMOTHY 1:13–2:2

*"The torch of heavenly light must be transmitted unquenched
from one generation to another."*

—*E. K. Simpson*

One of a soldier's highest honors is standing guard at the Tomb of the Unknown Soldier. If you've visited Arlington National Cemetery outside of Washington, D.C., you know how seriously each sentinel regards his task, as he honors those who have given their lives to protect America's freedom. They call their continuous march in front of the tomb "walking the mat."

The tomb has been guarded 24 hours a day, 7 days a week, since July 1937. Tomb Guards walk the mat in good weather and bad—stifling heat and bitter cold—without fail, without complaint, and without change of expression. While an emergency plan gives permission to retreat in case of severe weather, the sentinels have never budged.

On the night of September 18, 2003, Hurricane Isabel pounded the Capitol, but the Guard continued to walk the mat in front of the Tomb of the Unknown Soldier. For the first time ever, the sentinels were given permission to seek safety in the trophy room, out of fear the hurricane would become too dangerous.

None left.

Sergeant First Class Frederick Geary heard a sharp cracking sound, but he did not flinch as an old tree collapsed just two dozen yards from the plaza where he marched. Though the 60 + mph winds felled at least 24 trees that night, as sergeant of the guard, he led the charge to keep the sentinels on the black mat. "We made the decision to stand where we were," said Geary. Looking at the tomb of the unknowns, he choked up, "They did their job. We have a job to do here. I was just doing what I believed to be right."

Another sentinel, Sergeant Christopher Holmes insisted, "This is our highest honor."

In 2 Timothy 1:13–2:2, Paul writes to Timothy a message something like: "You have been entrusted with the highest honor—guarding the gospel. You stand as a sentinel outside an empty tomb that is the symbol of the gospel—Jesus Christ's victory over sin and the grave. Nothing is more valuable than this gospel. Guard it with your life! Even when the winds of change threaten or disastrous storms cause others to abandon their post, stand firm."

Paul has guarded the gospel given to him, and as he now passes the baton to Timothy, he challenges Timothy to hold the gospel tight. Timothy must not relax his grip, must not fumble, must not let it drop. Finishing well means guarding God's truth, and in this text, Paul describes three ways to guard the gospel.

# Through Doctrinal Defense

## Two Vivid Pictures

In 1:13-14, Paul uses two vivid expressions to describe the gospel. First, it is a "pattern" of sound teaching. The word for pattern—*hupotuposis*—has in it the idea of "an outline sketch such as an architect might make . . . of a building."[1] Timothy is not to allow anyone to "remodel" or "add on" to the gospel. He must ensure that the original apostolic blueprint is followed.

The second expression for the gospel is "the good deposit"—a *paratheke*. In ancient Greece, a man could deposit an inheritance with a friend to be kept for his children. He might deposit his valuables in a temple (the banks of the ancient world) for safekeeping. In each case the deposit was called a *paratheke*. William Barclay writes, "In the ancient world there was no more sacred duty than the safe-guarding of such a deposit and the returning of it when in due time it was claimed."[2]

Timothy, then, was to guard the gospel as a sacred treasure. In fact, the word "guard" is used elsewhere of guarding a palace against marauders and possessions against thieves (Luke 11:21; Acts 22:20). He must defend the gospel against the heretics in Ephesus who seek to spoil the treasure entrusted to him by God.

## Protecting the Flock

There is still a need today to defend the "pattern of sound teaching." Many—from both inside and outside the church—seek to corrupt the gospel. In one of the churches I served, a young couple became enamored with a popular televangelist. They watched his program, subscribed to his magazine, and sent money to his organization.

Unfortunately, this man was a false teacher. He taught that, when people become Christians, they can make things happen simply by speaking the words with enough faith. Just as God spoke things into existence, he said, so can we. This is sometimes called "name it and claim it" theology.

Sadly, the young couple in my congregation was deceived. They began to apply his teaching in how they ran their new business—seeking to make certain things happen by "speaking them in faith." I sat down in their living room to express my concerns, but my warning fell on deaf ears. When their business faltered, their faith did as well. Thankfully, they eventually realized their error and returned to the gospel.

The stakes are high here. Today the gospel is threatened by those who change its teaching on sexual ethics, Jesus' identity, the inspiration of Scripture, the sovereignty of God, salvation requirements, and many other topics. By the way, heresy can take at least two forms: requiring *less* than the gospel does and requiring *more* than the gospel does. Both permissiveness and legalism "remodel" the original apostolic blueprint, and we must confront such false teaching. Admittedly, this is a challenging task. It's always more enjoyable to teach the truth than to confront error, but sometimes confrontation is necessary, because souls are at stake.

Warren Wiersbe tells the story of a pastor who raised concerns about an unsavory business opening near a school. His protest led to a court case, and the defense attorney sought to embarrass the minister.

"Are you not a pastor," asked the lawyer. "And doesn't the word pastor mean shepherd?" The minister agreed. "Well if you're a shepherd, why aren't you out taking care of your sheep?"

The pastor replied, "Because today I'm fighting the wolves!"

In guarding the gospel, Timothy is protecting his flock.

## Through Personal Sacrifice

Guarding the gospel not only requires doctrinal defense; it also demands personal sacrifice. Standing up for the gospel carries a price—ridicule, rejection, even physical persecution—and sometimes we can be reluctant to pay.

### The Temptation to Wimp Out

I once spent a year working with Bob Russell, then senior minister of Southeast Christian Church in Louisville, Kentucky. Bob took bold stands on biblical truth, but he told of one time he took the easy way out. As a megachurch preacher, Bob was often asked to pray at community events. Once at a civic function, the organizer found him a few minutes before the invocation. "Remember that we have people from many different backgrounds here," she said.

Bob understood what she was asking: give a generic prayer to avoid offending those of other faiths. He began with "Dear Father"—safe ground because many religions use the term "Father." The problem, Bob knew, would be the ending. Because Jesus said, "My Father will give you whatever you ask in my name," Christians have traditionally closed their prayers with "in Jesus' name" (John 16:23).

Bob ended, "I pray these things in the name of the Lion of the Tribe of Judah, Amen." He sat down feeling smug—he had prayed in Jesus' name and almost nobody knew it! Reflecting back, Bob said, "Some might call that creativity, but I call that cowardice. I wimped out. After that, I decided I would always pray 'in Jesus' name.' I've noticed two results: I feel better about my witness, and I get fewer invitations to pray!"

The fact is: at best, identifying with Jesus can be unpopular. At worst, it can be downright dangerous. That was certainly true in the first century, and so Paul says, "everyone in the province of Asia has deserted me, including Phygelus and Hermogenes" (1:15). When Paul was arrested, many turned their backs on him and perhaps even on Christianity. Maybe they thought this new Christian cause was now lost. Whoever Phygelus and Hermogenes were, their betrayal apparently hurt Paul the worst.

> Identifying with Jesus can be unpopular at best or even dangerous.

## The Gospel Is Free, but Not Cheap

But thank the Lord, he at least had Onesiphorus. Onesiphorus was from Ephesus, where Paul had his longest recorded ministry, and over that time, these men had grown close. Onesiphorus loved Paul, had been a constant help to him, and had often opened his home to the apostle to refresh him with hospitality.

Though now Paul was a prisoner of Rome, Onesiphorus would not turn his back. He was a living example of the exhortation Paul had given to Timothy: "Do not be ashamed to testify about our Lord, or ashamed of me his prisoner" (1:8). He traveled the 1200 miles from Ephesus to Rome, and when he arrived in the great city, he tramped through the streets and alleys, government buildings and ghettoes, searching for Paul until he found him.

Understand: there was great risk in associating with an enemy of the Empire. As one commentator writes, "It was dangerous to keep asking where a certain criminal could be found; it was dangerous to visit him; it was still more dangerous to keep on visiting him; but that is what Onesiphorus did."[3] Why would Onesiphorus make such a personal sacrifice? Because of the bond he shared with Paul *in the gospel*. He was committed to

Paul because he was committed to Jesus. Sometimes the way we guard the gospel is simply by not letting go of it when the gospel is inconvenient or even risky.

Many have made personal sacrifices because they were unwilling to let the gospel be compromised:

- A Christian psychologist is fired after she declines to counsel a lesbian about her relationship.
- A university professor in Iowa loses his job because of his stand on the biblical view of creation.
- A Chinese pastor is imprisoned for preaching the truth about Jesus.
- A Christian in a Muslim country refuses to renounce his faith in Christ and is burned over an open flame.

Such sacrifice is demanding, but the good news is that we don't have to suffer in our own strength. In both 1:14 and 2:1, Paul reminds Timothy that the Spirit of Christ within him will give him the strength he needs.

At some point you may be called on to sacrifice for the sake of the gospel. Are you willing to pay the price? I once heard preacher Tom Ellsworth tell of visiting the Lincoln Memorial in Washington, D.C. He stopped at a souvenir stand across the street to check out the wares. He picked up a little bronze replica of the flag-raising memorial to the Marines who fought at Iwo Jima in WW2. The disinterested man behind the stand suddenly perked up, sensing a potential sale. "Cheap!" he said with a smile. "Only $10!"

Tom nodded, put the bronze replica back and walked on, thinking to himself, "No, not cheap. Not cheap at all." In 36 days of fighting, the Marines sustained over 25,000 casualties on Iwo Jima—including 7,000 fatalities. More Marines received the Medal of Honor for their service at Iwo Jima than for any other battle in U.S. history. There was nothing cheap about it. As Americans, these men received their freedom at no cost, but to defend that freedom, they paid a great price.

Likewise, as Christians we receive the gospel at no cost, but to defend that gospel, we may have to pay a great price. The gospel is free, but it is not cheap.

## Through Relational Investment

In 2 Timothy 2:2, Paul describes the third way Timothy is to guard the gospel—investing in the next generation of gospel teachers. He challenges Timothy to mentor future leaders: "And the things you have heard me say in the presence of many witnesses entrust to reliable men who will also be qualified to teach others."

## Links in a Living Chain

E.K. Simpson wrote, "The torch of heavenly light must be transmitted unquenched from one generation to another." Notice the stages in the faithful transmission of the gospel from one generation to the next:

- *The transmission from Christ to Paul.* In Galatians 1:10-11, Paul writes, "The gospel I preached . . . I received . . . by revelation from Jesus Christ."
- *The transmission from Paul to Timothy.* Timothy heard Paul teach the gospel "in the presence of many witnesses."
- *The transmission from Timothy to "reliable men."* Notice these must be men who can be counted on to guard the gospel.
- *The transmission from "reliable men" to "others."*

Of course, these "others" will also someday pass the gospel on to the next generation and so on, all the way to the present time. The one who stands up in your church next Sunday to teach "is a link in the living chain which stretches unbroken from this present moment back to Jesus Christ."[4]

This living chain is essential if we are to guard the truth of God's Word from one generation to the next. We must be highly intentional about training up the next wave of gospel leaders and teachers, because it is so easy for "truth decay" to happen in the generational exchange. As someone has said, "What one generation defends, the next assumes, and the next neglects." So how can this leadership mentoring take place?

## No Success without a Successor

First, *recognize that leadership training is a priority.* Someone has said there is no success without a successor. No matter how impressive your accomplishments, you have only "built to last" if you have prepared those who will continue the work when you are gone. As my high school track coach told my 4×800 relay team, "Races are won or lost at the passing of the baton."

That's why Jack Welch, the former CEO of General Electric, said that he spent 30% of his time doing leadership development with emerging leaders at GE. That's why we must spend significant time entrusting the work of the gospel to "reliable men." As the journalist Walter Lippman once wrote, "The final test of a leader is that he leaves behind in other men the conviction and will to carry on." Make this a priority.

Second, *look for potential future leaders.* They may be eloquent or slow of speech, five-talent-people or one-talent-people, A + or C- students. God has given the gifts of leadership and teaching to all kinds of people. The ability within them may not

> "The final test of a leader is that he leaves behind in other men the conviction and will to carry on."

yet be developed, so look closely for the raw material: Christian character, a sense of responsibility, an understanding of people, a desire to see the church reach its full potential. To whom do others listen? Who shows an earnestness about spiritual matters? Who is looking for opportunities to serve even without the label of "leader"?

By the way, don't forget about the young people in your congregation. Eighty-year-old D.P. Shaffer was still preaching in Conneautville, Pennsylvania, when he heard a first-grader quote a large portion of John 14 in front of the congregation. After the service, D.P. patted the boy's head and said, "You are going to make a good preacher someday." That little boy's name was Bob Russell, who never forgot those words and went on to lead Southeast Christian Church in Louisville, Kentucky. Keep an eye open for the students in your church who might be one of the "reliable men" someday, and plant those seed-thoughts.

Third, *build a relationship*. Paul invested deeply in his relationship with Timothy—just as Jesus did with His disciples. When you find "reliable men," get to know them, spend time with them, and genuinely care about them. Dr. Lynn Gardner was the academic dean at Ozark Christian College when I began teaching there. I was just 26 years old—barely shaving! I wasn't sure how I would be received by the other faculty, including some who had been there longer than I'd been alive. Thankfully, they welcomed me with open arms, and especially Dr. Gardner. He once said to me, "The way I figure it, we're supposed to be more like the old horse than the old dog. The old dog is afraid the young dog will get his bone, but the old horse is glad for the young horse because he can help carry the load."

Dr. Gardner sure acted like he was glad I was there. He made a point to talk to me in the hallway or in the library. He'd go out of his way to pass on little pieces of wit and wisdom, recommend a good book to me, or tell me a story of his early teaching days. After I preached in chapel, Dr. Gardner told me he appreciated my sermon. When I was staying too many hours on campus that first year of teaching, he encouraged me to go home and be with my family.

I knew he cared, so I listened when he spoke. A mentor will build a relationship.

Fourth, *teach them what you know*. If you're a preacher, teach them how to write a sermon. If you're an elder, take them with you on a hospital call. If you're a Sunday School teacher, show them how you prepare a lesson. Get them involved with you and look for opportunities to share what you've learned through the years about Scripture and life. Talk to them about the essentials of the faith, and study the Bible together. Urge them to remain true to the gospel.

Leonard Ravenhill tells of a tourist in a European village who asked a local, "Were any great men born in this village?" The local replied, "Nope. Only babies." The fact is: leaders are made, not born. Leaders don't suddenly appear fully developed. They will have to be taught. As you teach them, you are guarding the gospel by ensuring its preservation and proclamation in the next generation.

## An Unlikely Looking Sentinel

For thirty-five years, Henrietta Mears taught the college Sunday school class at the large First Presbyterian Church in Hollywood, California. Five-foot-four-inches tall, thickset, with "coke-bottle" glasses and a deep love for Christ, this passionate woman sent out over 400 young men and women into Christian service, including eventual U.S. Senate Chaplain Richard Halverson, Young Life founder Jim Rayburn, and Campus Crusade for Christ founder Bill Bright.

At one point a young, largely unknown evangelist named Billy Graham sought out Miss Mears. The winds of liberal theology were howling in the late 1940s, and one of Billy's closest evangelist friends had abandoned his belief in the infallibility of Scripture. Billy was questioning what he himself believed.

Though Henrietta looked nothing like one of the sentinels at the Tomb of the Unknown Soldier, she held her ground just as staunchly as the guards during Hurricane Isabel. She talked to Billy about reasons for believing in the Bible's infallibility. She refused to compromise or conform to current theological thought. Her gentle but strong convictions made a deep impression on young Graham as he stood at a faith crossroads, and he decided that he too would hold to orthodox Christianity. It was immediately after that decision that Billy Graham's Los Angeles crusade catapulted him to worldwide recognition and ministry. Praise God for a five-foot-four-inch-tall defender of the faith named Henrietta!

The truth is too important, the stakes are too high, the threat is too real for us to abandon our post. Stand strong when the storms of doubt and error rage. You have been entrusted with a high and sacred honor.

Guard the gospel. 3:16

---

[1] Donald Guthrie, *The Pastoral Epistles* (Leicester, England: Inter-Varsity; Grand Rapids: Eerdmans, 1990) 145.

[2] William Barclay, *The Letters to Timothy, Titus and Philemon* (Philadelphia: Westminster/John Knox, 1975) 151.

[3] Ibid., 156.

[4] Ibid., 158.

*Guard the Truth*

# Going On When We Feel Like Giving In

1. What do you think are essential elements of the gospel? What are the nonnegotiables of the Christian faith?

2. What do you think is the greatest threat to the content of the gospel in our culture? Where is our culture seeking to undermine the clear teaching of Scripture?

3. Have you ever come into contact with false teaching? What was it? How did you respond? How could you have responded?

4. In what ways might we have to personally sacrifice for the sake of the gospel?

5. How intentional is your congregation about training up the next generation of leaders? Have you sent anyone into the ministry recently? Does your church have any kind of biblical or theological training for upcoming leaders (elders, deacons, teachers, etc.)?

6. What could you personally do to help raise up the next generation of "reliable men who will also be qualified to teach others?"

7. Ask God for the courage to stand firm for the gospel's truth.

**Memory Verse**
2 Tim 1:14

*Guard the good deposit that was entrusted to you—guard it with the help of the Holy Spirit who lives in us.*

CHAPTER SIX

# EXPECT TOUGH TIMES

## 2 TIMOTHY 2:3-13

*"Stick-to-it-iveness is an important Christian virtue. As one preacher used to say, 'There are three abilities: know-ability, do-ability and stick-ability. And the greatest of these is stick."*

—*Seth Wilson*

Whuman the going gets tough, the tough get going." Or so the saying goes. More often, however, we simply want the tough going to go away. A few years ago, hikers in the Bridger-Teton National Forest left the following actual comments in a suggestion box:

- Trail needs to be reconstructed. Please avoid building trails that go uphill.
- Too many bugs and leeches and spiders and spider webs. Please spray the wilderness to rid the area of these pests.
- Chairlifts need to be installed so we can get to wonderful views without having to hike to them.
- Please pave the trails. Too many rocks in the mountains.
- A small deer came into my camp and stole my jar of pickles. Is there a way I can get reimbursed?

Sometimes we are, as one book title suggests, "a nation of wimps." Let's face it—the natural human response to suffering is to avoid it. In Mark 4:16-17, Jesus predicted that, when the going got tough for some new Christians, they would want to quit. When trouble or persecution comes because of the word, they quickly fall away. When these believers discover that Christianity isn't easy, they drop out.

In 2 Timothy 2:3-13, Paul wants Timothy to know two things: the Christian life is *really hard* . . . and *really worth it*.

# The Pictures of Endurance

Paul begins with three metaphors that Timothy is to "reflect on" (2:7). Warren Wiersbe says the human mind is not a debating hall; it's a picture gallery. We most often think in pictures, images, metaphors—and those metaphors matter, because we act in alignment with these images.

I once read an article in a psychology journal entitled "Clergy Stress and Role Metaphors" which linked a minister's stress to how he pictures his role. In a survey, ministers were asked to fill in the blank: "A pastor is like a _____." They answered with a variety of images—ship captain, gardener, CEO, shepherd, coach, and others.

The results suggested that some metaphors lead to greater stress than others. Metaphors carry expectations. If a minister's experience didn't fit his mental expectations, he could become disillusioned and discouraged. If you think ministry is more like gardening than soldiering, then, when bullets start flying, you might abandon your post and go AWOL.

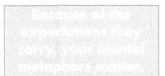

The point is: your mental metaphors matter. That's why Stuart Briscoe says, "If we spent more time telling people *who* they are, we wouldn't have to spend as much time telling them *what* to do." So in 2:3-6, Paul tells Timothy who he is, using three "role metaphors." The apostle hangs three images in Timothy's mental picture gallery, and each one carries with it some expectation of difficulty.

## Soldier

In 2:3, Paul compares Timothy to a soldier. Paul knew something about Roman soldiers, having spent a considerable portion of his life guarded by them! He knew that a Roman soldier was a picture of complete dedication. There were no "weekend warriors"—they were required to sign on for a 20-year hitch. They were forbidden to marry in order to avoid civilian distractions (2:4). Only half of all Roman soldiers survived to retirement, so every soldier knew to expect hardship. This was no 9-5 job. A Roman soldier ate, drank, breathed, slept, lived, and died doing his duty as a soldier.

In fact, the word "endure" in 2:3 was a military word used to describe a soldier holding position. *Hupomone*—literally "remain under"—meant stay at your post, stand your ground, stick to your guns. When the eruption of Mt. Vesuvius destroyed the Italian city of Pompeii in A.D. 79, many people were immediately buried in the volcanic ash, preserved in their final frozen moment of terror. Amazingly, a Roman sentinel was found at the city gate, his hands still grasping his weapon. He had been placed there by his captain, and though the earth shook beneath him, as the fiery rain of ashes overwhelmed him, he stood at his post. There he was found standing a thousand years later—faithful even in death. That's *hupomone*.

A soldier doesn't know the word "quit." Some believers today are like the kamikaze pilot who flew 50 missions. (Think about that.) They want to be involved, but not committed. As someone said, "Too many Christians want the medals, but they don't want the scars."

I want to be a soldier like Art Chen. Art Chen was a Chinese fighter pilot in the 1930s when China was at war with Japan. In one battle, Art Chen took on three Japanese fighter planes. He shot one down, then ran out of ammunition, so he deliberately rammed a second plane, disabling it and then parachuting out of his own plane. He landed close to the wreckage of his plane and managed to salvage one of the heavy machine guns from his plane.

Art Chen hoisted the heavy gun up on his shoulder and carried it eight miles back to his air base. When he arrived, Art found his commanding officer, dropped the big gun in front of him, and said, "Sir, can I have another airplane for my machine gun?"

That's a soldier who doesn't know the word "quit." Paul says, "Timothy, that's who you are. When you look in the mirror, that's a soldier looking back. Soldiers expect hardship, and soldiers don't quit."

> When you look in the mirror, that's a soldier looking back.

## Athlete

In 2:5, Paul compares Timothy to an athlete. Paul was apparently a sports fan and often used athletic imagery to picture the Christian life—including running (Gal 2:2), boxing (1 Cor 9:26), wrestling (Eph 6:12), gladiatorial contests (1 Cor 4:9), and chariot races (Phil 3:13-14). Here Paul says that an athlete "competes according to the rules" (2:5). That phrase refers to the oath every Olympic athlete had to take, pledging to enter ten months of strict training before the Games. Before these athletes could win the crown, they had to push themselves through the suffering. An athlete understood that hardship was part of the package.

It's still true today. Athletes push themselves with the motto, "No pain, no gain." (My personal motto is "No pain, no pain.") They expect difficulty. When a running back gets tackled, he doesn't get up whining to the opposing player, "What did you do that for? Nobody told me I was going to get hit." If you're a football player, you know that if you carry the ball, you're going to get tackled.

Paul's point is that Christians ought to expect difficulty as well. First Peter 4:12 says, "Don't be surprised by the fiery trial you are now going through as though something strange were happening to you." Second Timothy 3:12 promises that "everyone who wants to live a godly life in Christ Jesus will be persecuted." If you thought becoming a Christian would solve all your problems, think again. Hardship is part of the pack-

age. But as spiritual athletes, we push through it. We run all the way across the finish line.

I'm a sucker for courageous sports stories—tales of athletes who heroically persevere through pain. Maybe you'll remember these:

- After his jaw was broken, Muhammad Ali fought 10 more rounds, finishing a bout with Ken Norton.
- Kirk Gibson hit a walk-off homer to win Game 1 of the 1988 World Series despite a badly-pulled hamstring.
- In the 1997 NBA Finals Game 5, Michael Jordan's severe flu made him look like death warmed over, but he scored 38 points including the game-winning basket.
- Kerry Strug clinched the team gymnastics gold medal for the U.S. in the 1996 Olympics by vaulting with an injured ankle.

Paul is saying to Timothy and to you, "This is who you are. When you look in the mirror, that's an athlete looking back. Athletes expect hardship, and athletes don't quit."

### Farmer

Paul also compares Timothy to a farmer (2:6). I have worked on a farm, and it can be hard physical labor, long hours, heavy loads. But think: Paul is writing before the days of air-conditioned tractor cabs and hydraulic forklifts. A farmer in the ancient world lived an even more difficult life. Paul calls him "hardworking," and that word *kopiao* pictures sweat and struggle, bent back and straining muscles, exertion and exhaustion. As John Stott points out, "unlike the soldier and the athlete, the farmer's life is totally devoid of excitement, remote from all glamour of peril and of applause."[1]

But a farmer knew that if he didn't work, his family didn't eat. So, hard as it was, a farmer didn't quit. He kept working. While *kopiao* usually referred to manual labor, Paul elsewhere uses it to describe the spiritual work of a Christian. In Romans 16:6, he mentions "Mary who has *worked hard* for you." In 1 Timothy 5:17, he mentions elders "whose *work* is preaching and teaching." In 2 Corinthians 6:5, Paul lists his leadership credentials as "beatings, imprisonments and riots . . . *hard work*, sleepless nights and hunger."

Such persistent work is part of being a Christian and a Christian leader. Paul is saying, "This is who you are. When you look in the mirror, that's a farmer looking back. Farmers expect hardship, and farmers don't quit."

# The Purposes of Endurance

By the way, with each of these three metaphors, Paul hints at a reward for endurance. A soldier gets a medal after pleasing his commanding officer (2:4). An athlete wins a crown after competing according to the rules (2:5). A farmer reaps a harvest after working hard in the fields (2:6).

In other words, Paul is saying that the Christian life is *really hard . . .* and *really worth it.*

He wants to remind us that we do not labor in vain. Joe Namath, the famous New York Jets quarterback, once said, "When you're winning, nothing hurts." We endure hardship more readily when we recognize some worthwhile purpose behind it. As Viktor Frankl, the Jewish psychiatrist and Holocaust survivor, wrote, "'He who has a *why* to live can bear with almost any *how*."

So what exactly is the *why* of the Christian life? What is the reward for enduring difficult times? What purposes does it accomplish? In 2:8-13, Paul mentions at least three reasons for persevering.

> We endure hardship more readily when we recognize some worthwhile purpose behind it.

## You Become More Like Christ

Maybe you've heard the story of the two little boys at the breakfast table. Kevin was 8, Ryan was 5, and they were fighting over who would get the first pancake. Seeing a teachable moment, their mother sat down and said, "You know, if Jesus were sitting here, He would say, 'Let my brother have the first pancake.'" So Kevin turned to his little brother and said, "Okay, Ryan . . . you be Jesus!"

As Christians, we say we want to be like Jesus, but are we willing to endure hardship to see it happen? In 2:8, Paul writes, "Remember Jesus Christ, raised from the dead, descended from David." Notice the order of those last two phrases. Before he mentions the kingship of Christ ("descended from David"), Paul mentions the cross of Christ ("raised from the *dead*"). Before the crown of gold came the crown of thorns. Before Christ's sovereignty came His suffering. Paul is reminding Timothy that Jesus Himself had to endure hard times. So when we endure hardships, we are becoming like Jesus.

The ancient Christian writer Tertullian said, "The man who is afraid to suffer cannot belong to Him who suffered." Jesus Himself said in John 15:20, "No servant is greater than his master. If they persecuted me, they will persecute you also." If we choose to walk in the footsteps of Jesus, we will wind up walking up a hill to a cross. As someone said, "If you want to follow Jesus, you'd better look good on wood."

When we live lives of sacrifice, it not only *connects* us to the experience of Christ, but it *conforms* us to the character of Christ. The simple act of persevering can grow us toward spiritual maturity. James 1:4 says, "Let perseverance finish its work so that you may be mature and complete, not lacking anything."[2]

In one of his books, John Ortberg mentions a survey in which "hundreds of people were asked to identify the factors that were most formative in their spiritual growth. The number one response overwhelmingly involved times of suffering and pain."[3] A few weeks ago, I spoke with a man whose son died of a terrible disease at age 15. He said, "If I had it to do over, I would not have wanted this tragedy to happen, but neither would I want to be the man I was before it happened."

The act of holding onto Jesus through painful times draws us closer to Him, so don't quit.

## You Bring People to Christ

A second purpose for endurance is that God may use your steadfastness to bring people to Himself. In 2:9-10, Paul says that he is "suffering even to the point of being chained like a criminal, but . . . I endure everything for the sake of the elect, that they too may obtain the salvation that is in Christ Jesus, with eternal glory." Paul is willing to endure trials if, by so doing, he can help introduce people to Jesus.

Sometimes the greatest witness to a lost world is not persuasive oratory, ironclad evidences or dramatic testimony. It is simply a life lived faithfully, through good times and bad, over the long haul.

One of my students preaches in Irwin, Missouri, population 35. The Irwin church is just a handful of loyal saints, including Thelma. Thelma is almost 90, hard of hearing, and can't get out when it's colder than 45 degrees. But Thelma hasn't retired from service.

When Thelma heard that her neighbor Denise was diagnosed with lupus, she baked a plate of cookies and slowly walked down the street to Denise's house. Because of Thelma's simple act of compassion, Denise is now a part of the Irwin church—and so are Denise's family members Daniel, A.J., Amanda, Isaac, Jacob, and Debbie. Thelma's loving witness almost doubled the church's membership!

Thelma can't do much now at 90, but one thing she won't do is quit. Sometimes it's not the wattage of our light that makes the difference. It's just the fact that it keeps on shining no matter what happens. You don't have to be a halogen floodlight. God can work through 25-watt people who just refuse to burn out.

So, Paul is saying, we "endure everything" in order to win some. Timothy must keep loving, keep serving, keep working, keep praying, keep speaking, keep persevering, keep shining because, somewhere along the line, God might use something Timothy does to usher someone into the kingdom.

You never know: He might use something *you* do, so don't quit.

## You Save Your Seat with Christ

In verses 11-13, Paul quotes what he calls "a trustworthy saying." This is one of five "trustworthy sayings" scattered through the Pastoral Epistles (1 Tim 1:15; 3:1; 4:9, and Titus 3:8). These sayings were apparently creeds or hymns often used in the early church—material already familiar to the apostle's readers.

This ancient hymn contains four stanzas, each starting with the word "if," and each stanza focuses on God's response to a different situation.

- The first stanza is God's response to a believer's *conversion.* "If we died with him" refers to our death with Christ in the waters of baptism (see Rom 6:4). When we make the initial choice to follow Christ, God gives us the hope of new life, both in this world and the world to come.

- The second stanza is God's response to a believer's *endurance.* If, after that initial decision, we remain true to Christ, God will welcome us into heaven someday and allow us to reign alongside Christ forever. Wow! I'll return to this theme in a moment.

- The third stanza is God's response to a believer's *disavowal.* When a believer finally and fully turns his back on God, God has no choice but to turn His back finally as well. This is the same kind of warning Jesus gave in Matthew 10:33, "Whoever disowns me before men, I will disown him before my Father in heaven."

- The fourth stanza is God's response to a believer's *failure.* "Faithless" here does not refer to a complete lack of faith, but a wavering faith (see Mark 9:24). Stanza 3 dealt with a person's permanent rejection of God, but this fourth stanza deals with a believer's temporary lapse into disobedience. If stanza 3 describes Judas's once-for-all betrayal, stanza 4 describes Peter's momentary denial. God promises here to be faithful to such a person, despite their failings. As 1 John 1:9 says, "If we confess our sins, he is faithful and just and will forgive us our sins and purify us from all unrighteousness." If a prodigal son returns, God welcomes him back with open arms.

The big idea of the hymn is simply this: God sticks by those who stick by Him. What exactly does God do for those who endure? He saves them a seat with Him in heaven someday. By the way, that seat is a throne! The promise of 2:12 is that we will reign with Christ forever.[4] Though now on this earth we are sometimes outcasts, in heaven we shall be royalty.

God sticks by those who stick by Him.

When my daughter Lydia was 5, she wanted desperately to be royalty. Lydia's kindergarten teacher made a photo album of her students, and each child's page included their answers to a list of questions. One question was, "What do you want to be when you grow up?" The other children's answers were predictable: doctor, teacher, nurse, truck driver. Lydia, however, was the only one who answered, "Queen."

She loved dressing up in gowns and crowns, swishing around the house, receiving the applause of her adoring subjects. Lydia couldn't watch enough of those Disney movies like *Sleeping Beauty* and *Cinderella* and *Beauty and the Beast*—movies where the princess swirls around the ballroom, dances with the prince, marries him, and lives happily ever after. She really wanted to be royalty.

She's older now, but I don't ever want her to lose that.

I know that as Lydia grows up, she will go through hard times. The going will get tough. She will face trials and tribulations, and at some point, she will feel like giving up.

But I want her to know that someday, if she holds on, she will inherit a kingdom more wealthy than any earthly kingdom.

She will live in a palace more beautiful than Disney could ever draw.

At the wedding banquet of the Lamb, she will not just dance with the prince. If she endures, she will get to dance with the King Himself.

And so will you. So don't quit.

The Christian life is really hard . . . and *really worth it*. 

---

[1] Stott, *Message of 2 Timothy*, 56.
[2] Author's translation.
[3] Ortberg, *Life You've Always Wanted*, 208.
[4] For the idea of reigning with Christ, see Matt 19:28; Luke 22:30; Rom 5:17; Rev 3:21; 5:10; 20:4; and 22:5.

# Going On When We Feel Like Giving In

1. Do you agree or disagree with the statement "when the going gets tough, we want the tough going to go away"? Give examples.

2. Finish the sentence: "Being a Christian is like being a _____." What is your mental metaphor of the Christian life? What expectations come with your mental metaphor? Which of the three metaphors Paul used can you most identify with—soldier, athlete, farmer?

3. Enduring hardship can help make you more like Christ. Have you ever experienced spiritual growth because of a time of suffering or pain? How?

4. In what ways could enduring hardship help bring other people to Christ? Can you think of an example?

5. In 2:13, "faithless" does not mean a complete lack of faith, but a wavering faith, like Peter when he denied Christ. Have you ever had a wavering faith or experienced a moment of failure like Peter did? How did you feel afterward? God has promised to welcome us back when we stumble. In what ways does knowing this affect how you view your failure?

6. Rate your endurance level at the moment on a scale of 1-10, where 1 is ready to walk off the track and 10 is running strong. Ask God to give you the strength to move further up the scale. Thank Him for the promise of faithfulness when we stumble.

> **Memory Verse**
> 2 Tim 2:2-3
>
> *And the things you have heard me say in the presence of many witnesses entrust to reliable men who will also be qualified to teach others. ³Endure hardship with us like a good soldier of Christ Jesus.*

CHAPTER SEVEN

# MAINTAIN YOUR CHARACTER

## 2 TIMOTHY 2:14-26

*"It is not great talent God blesses so much as great likeness to Jesus. A holy minister is an awful weapon in the hand of God."*
*—Robert Murray McCheyne*

An old Arabic proverb says, "Choose your enemies wisely, for you may become them."

The proverb is right. When you oppose someone, there is a great danger of subtly taking on that person's qualities. If your enemy uses sarcasm, you may become sarcastic yourself. If your enemy exaggerates and conceals, you may start to rationalize such behavior of your own. If your enemy is insulting and rude, you may begin to act that way, too. After all, you're just "fighting fire with fire."

Walter Liefeld tells of a Christian apologist who debated famous atheists like Madeline Murray O'Hare, who sneered at Christian faith. Liefeld writes, "After one such appearance, some were troubled by this man's combative, demeaning attitude to the antagonist. His response was, 'I did not go there to save souls but to destroy a heretic.' I believe the apostle Paul would have hoped rather to destroy heresy and save a soul."[1]

"Choose your enemies wisely, for you may become them."

In 2:14-26, Paul tells Timothy to confront the false teachers in Ephesus because he is concerned about the dangerous effect of their teaching. But mostly Paul wants to ensure that, in the very act of opposing the false teachers, Timothy will not become like them. If he is to finish well someday, he must maintain a distinctly Christian character.

To describe this character, Paul again uses three metaphors. In 2:1-13, the three metaphors (soldier, athlete, farmer) pictured how to deal with difficult circumstances. In 2:14-26, the three metaphors (workman, instrument, servant) picture how to deal with difficult people.

# Maintain the Integrity of a Workman

The first metaphor Paul uses is that of a workman (2:15). If the church is like a building, then these false teachers are pulling it down, not building it up. In 2:14, when Paul says these false teachers are causing "ruin," he uses the Greek word *katastrophe*, a word that could be used for the demolition of a house. These guys are the wrong kind of workmen. In this text, we learn something about the false teachers' *identity, teaching content,* and *effects.*

## False Teaching Is Destructive

First their *identity*: Paul mentions Hymenaeus and Philetus by name (2:17). Likely this is the same Hymenaeus mentioned in 1 Timothy 1:20. Notice they are Greek names—that'll be important in a moment.

What is the *content* of their teaching? Verse 18 says they "say that the resurrection has already taken place." Of course, the hope of every Christian is a physical resurrection when Christ returns. In the new heavens and new earth, we'll have a new body. (I personally believe I'll be 6′3″, have a full head of hair, and finally be able to dunk a basketball.) In 1 Corinthians 15, Paul says the hope of physical resurrection is at the heart of our faith.

These false teachers, however, deny this hope. Instead, they teach that Christians are *spiritually* resurrected at baptism, but will never be *physically* resurrected. "You got a new heart in the past," they tell believers, "but there is no new body in the future."

It is certainly true that we're spiritually resurrected at baptism (Rom 6:4), but why deny the physical resurrection? Because of Greek dualism. A prevalent Greek belief was that reality was composed of two substances: the physical and the spiritual. The physical was by nature corrupt, whereas the spiritual was by nature good. Many, specifically the Stoics, sought to deny their body, because it was inherently evil. (See 1 Tim 4:3.) They even used a play on words to summarize their view—*"soma sema"*—which meant "the body is a tomb."

So the last thing a Greek wanted was to live in a body for all eternity. (Remember that Hymenaeus and Philetus are Greek names.) Apparently, these false teachers had watered down the Christian gospel—compromising to accommodate their culture. By the way, that still happens today:

- To accommodate a materialistic culture, some preach a "health and wealth" gospel.
- To accommodate a permissive culture, some preach homosexuality as acceptable to God.
- To accommodate a pluralistic culture, some preach Jesus as *a* way to God, but not *the* way to God.

*Maintain Your Character*

What are the *effects* of such false teaching? Paul vividly describes the results. It "ruins those who listen" (2:14). "Those who indulge in it become more and more ungodly" (2:16). It will "spread like gangrene" (2:17). It will "destroy the faith of some" (2:18).

In other words, it's dangerous and destructive. I heard about a Sunday School teacher who asked her class, "What is false doctrine?" One little boy raised his hand and said, "It's when the doctor gives the wrong stuff to people who are sick." Although the little boy had obviously confused *doctrine* with *doctorin'*, he still arrived at the correct definition. These false teachers were giving the wrong stuff and endangering people's eternal lives.

## Accurate Teaching Is Essential

Timothy must confront these false teachers and "warn them before God," solemnly charging them to knock it off. In the process, however, Timothy must avoid "becoming like the enemy." His opponents play fast and loose with Scripture, but Timothy must maintain his integrity as a "workman who does not need to be ashamed and who correctly handles the word of truth" (2:15).

By the way, Paul himself was a workman—a tentmaker by trade (Acts 18:3). Question: do you think he made sloppy tents? My hunch is that  Paul's tents were known for their excellent workmanship (Col 3:23). So here's an interesting note: the word for "correctly handles" literally means "to cut straight." Paul is telling Timothy to handle the Scripture like Paul handled his leather-knife—straight and true.

The call here is for painstaking accuracy when it comes to teaching Scripture. To maintain the integrity of a workman, Timothy must not compromise even a little. We must not be sloppy in studying Scripture. With some things in life, we can settle for "close enough," but other things demand 100% accuracy. If 99.9% were close enough for maternity wards, then 12 babies would go home every day from the hospital with the *wrong parents*. Some things you just have to get right.

The Bible is one of those things. God has taken care to communicate with us in words that can be clearly translated, grammatically diagrammed, contextually studied, and personally understood. He chose certain things to say and not say, particular words to use and not use, and we honor God when we pay careful attention to them. Others may be sloppy workmen, whose careless teaching tears down those around them. We are called to be workmen of integrity, building up those around us with careful biblical teaching.

# Maintain the Purity of a Noble Instrument

The second metaphor Paul uses is that of an "instrument"—a household utensil (2:20-21). Every household contains both noble instruments (silver pitcher and fine china) and nasty instruments (slop bucket and toilet plunger). In the same way, the Church contains both genuine believers and imitation believers. On Judgment Day, God will sort out the good from the bad, the wheat from the weeds, the sheep from the goats (Matt 13:24-30; 25:31-46).

But, Timothy may wonder, what if God mistakes him for one of the nasty instruments? Will he fall under God's judgment? Paul reassures Timothy (and the Ephesian church overhearing this letter) with a quotation from Numbers 16:5, "The Lord knows those who are his." Paul pictures this as an inscription on the foundation stone of the Church, alongside another inscription which calls believers to lives of holiness: "Everyone who confesses the name of the Lord must turn away from wickedness." Notice that these two inscriptions capture the two sides of salvation—God's and man's. The first is an encouragement, emphasizing *God's assurance* of salvation; the second is an exhortation, describing *our expression* of salvation.

So while we rest in God's promise, we must still pursue God's purity. The false teachers have given themselves over to impurity and wickedness. (See 2 Tim 3:1-9.) Timothy must not "become like his enemies." Instead of a slop bucket crusted in filth, he must be a clean vessel, a noble instrument for God's use.

> While we rest in God's promise, we must still pursue God's purity.

## "Run For Your Life!"

How exactly is Timothy to be a pure instrument for God's use? Paul gives Timothy two strategies. The first strategy is to run from sin. Paul writes, "Flee the evil desires of youth" (2 Tim 2:22). A man came to an old country doctor, saying, "Doc, I broke my arm in two places. What should I do?" The old doctor said, "You ought to stay out of them places!" Paul is charging Timothy to stay out of the places where a spiritual fall might occur.

Because Timothy was a single young man with normal sexual temptations, he probably had to avoid certain streets in Ephesus. The Temple of Artemis the fertility goddess may have included temple prostitutes, and archaeologists have uncovered, directly across the courtyard from the city library, the Ephesus town brothel. In fact, engravings in the marble street pavement show the way! Timothy is to avoid such places. Like Joseph in Genesis 39, he must run.

This is wise advice, no matter what sin you struggle with. Too many of us make too much provision for temptation for too long. We must not linger in the presence of temptation. As one preacher put it, "If we hesitate, we contemplate. If we contemplate, we negotiate. If we negotiate, we participate. If we participate, we devastate." Too many Christians never make it to the finish line because of moral failure.

Instead, we must flee. The Greek word for "flee" in 2:22 is where we derive the English word *fugitive*. We must run like a hunted man from lust, greed, anger, pride, laziness, and every other form of wickedness. As Paul tells Timothy in his first letter, "Run for your life from all this" (1 Tim 6:11, *The Message*). The first step to resisting temptation is *removing* temptation.

## Pursuing Righteousness with a Vengeance

Removing temptation, however, is not enough. The second step to resisting temptation is *replacing* temptation. Randy Alcorn writes, "Our minds are not vacuums. They will be filled with something. Impure thoughts are pushed out by pure thoughts."[2] The fact is: We must not simply remove evil desire. We must replace it with good. (See Matt 12:43-45.) That's why, after Paul says to "flee the evil desires of youth," he says to "pursue righteousness, faith, love and peace" (2:22).

If the first strategy was to run from sin, the second strategy is to chase after goodness. Christians are not simply to be known for what we *don't*

do—"we don't drink, smoke, chew, or go with girls who do." Ultimately Christians are to be known for what we *do*—acts of justice and love and peace. Are we actively engaged in developing the character of Jesus? It is not enough to run from the things of the devil; we must also run after the things of Christ.

In fact, the word for "pursue" is most often translated in the New Testament as "persecute." It means *to hunt down with a vengeance.* Paul is calling Timothy to pursue these character qualities with an intense intentionality—with a vengeance. He mustn't let a day go by without seeking to grow his love and peace and faith, without adding to their muscle, without checking to see if he is making progress.

Question: do you check your spiritual progress? When I was a kid, my dad would mark my height on the basement wall. Each year I could visibly see my growth. If there was a spiritual growth chart on your wall, would you have grown at all since last year? How intentional are you about your spiritual development program?

We must constantly evaluate where we need to grow in Christ—is it in developing loving relationships or exercising gentleness or being marked by joy or practicing self-control? Then we must actively engage in growing. If I am not a person of joy, for example, then I should strategize ways to grow in joy:

- Memorize Scriptures about joy.
- Hang around children—they are so good at joy.
- Make time in my schedule to slow down and enjoy God's creation.
- Learn a new joke and tell it three times this week.
- Sing.
- Pray that God will infect me with His joy.

This is what the active pursuit of righteousness looks like. Be intentional. As Timothy cultivates his own likeness to Jesus, he will be a noble instrument for God's use, "an awful weapon in the hand of God."

## Maintain the Humility of a Servant

The false teachers Timothy must face are proud, full of hot air, and attack this young man with criticism. It would be very easy to attack back. Evangelist Dwight L. Moody once received a note containing a single word: "Fool." Moody said he'd received many critical letters where the writer left off his name, but this was the first time the writer had left off the message and signed his name!

But Timothy must not become like his enemies by retaliating. In 2:24, Timothy is to respond by being "kind"—a word used of a nurse taking care of her children (1 Thess 2:7). In 2:24, he must maintain a spirit that is "not resentful"—which could be translated "patient with difficult people" (NLT).

In fact, the last metaphor Paul uses to describe Timothy's character is a "servant," or actually, a slave. The word is *doulos*—the "lowest term in the scale of servitude." Specifically, he is called "the Lord's *doulos*." This metaphor serves as a reminder of two important truths:

- Timothy is not as important as what he might be tempted to think.
- God is the one who will ultimately defend him, since he belongs to the Lord.

These reminders are incredibly freeing. While the false teachers' pride expressed itself in arrogant argument and defensive quarrels, Timothy could be free from these. Instead, he could "gently instruct, in the hope that God will grant them repentance leading them to a knowledge of the truth" (2:25). Timothy can offer correction in a nonangry, nondefensive, humble spirit.

### How Can I Humbly Correct When Needed?

When we need to confront, one way to maintain humility is through *gentle humor*. Grady Wilson, a member of Billy Graham's evangelistic team, was known for his sense of humor. He liked to tell the story of the time he and Billy Graham were received by the Archbishop of Canterbury, who was not terribly enamored of American evangelists. The Archbishop asked Graham how he and his party had traveled to Great Britain. Billy said they had come over on the *Queen Elizabeth*. Objecting to the seeming luxury, the

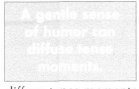

Archbishop stiffly replied, "Well, you know, our Lord entered Jerusalem on a lowly donkey." Grady Wilson replied with a smile, "Well, Archbishop, if you can find me a donkey that can swim the Atlantic, we'll take it!" A gentle sense of humor can diffuse tense moments.

When we seek to correct wrong teaching, another way to maintain humility is through *respectful sensitivity*. Ravi Zacharias, a well-known apologist, tells of speaking at a university in Thailand about existentialism, Marxism, and Christianity. A Muslim stood up and said, "You have just insulted your God by mentioning Karl Marx and Jean Paul Sartre in the same sentence that you mentioned Christ."

Ravi could feel the irritation welling up inside him and wanted to retort, "I have done nowhere near what the Muslim world has done in stripping Christ of his deity." Instead, he paused, took a drink of water, and said, "I deeply appreciate your sensitivity. I know where you are coming from. But don't forget you also used all three names in the sentence as you raised the question for me. Did you mean to equate them by naming the three of them?"

"No," he said.

"Neither did I," replied Ravi. "Mentioning two names in the same sentence is hardly suggesting they are equal. But I want to commend you for your sensitivity because in many cultures we have lost reverence for the name of God."

We must correct wrongheaded beliefs in a way that encourages people to listen when we offer them the truth of Christianity. We must be bold enough to correct, but if we are harsh and unkind, they'll tune us out when we get to the gospel. The old Indian proverb holds true: "Once you've cut off a person's nose, there's no point giving him a rose to smell."

One last reminder when confronting: *remember who the real enemy is*. It's true that when confronting these false teachers, Timothy must not "become like his enemies." But the fact is: the real enemy is Satan. In 2:26, Paul says that Timothy's opponents have actually been taken captive by the devil. Though they oppose the true gospel, at the end of the day they are prisoners of war, not enemies. They are victims of our real nemesis. When we remember this, we will seek not simply to win the argument. We will seek to win their souls.

As we maintain integrity, purity, and humility, may we see our enemies return to the side of God. 🔲

---

[1] Walter Liefeld, *1 & 2 Timothy/Titus* (Grand Rapids: Zondervan, 1999) 267.

[2] Randy Alcorn, *The Purity Principle* (Nashville: LifeWay Press, 2001) 45-46.

# Going On When We Feel Like Giving In

1. The chapter started with a proverb: "Choose your enemies wisely for you may become them." Have you ever seen an example of this?

2. Rate your Bible knowledge on a scale of 1-10, with 10 being a biblical expert and 1 being in biblical kindergarten. How well do you think you could tell the difference between Bible and "almost Bible"?

3. In what ways could you become a better Bible student?

4. Paul told Timothy to run for his life from temptation. What makes this difficult in our culture? How could we become more serious and more intentional about avoiding temptation?

5. If you are going to "pursue righteousness with a vengeance," you will want to develop a spiritual development program. What virtues do you especially need to grow in your life? What are some specific ways that you could cultivate that characteristic? In what ways could you measure your growth in that area in, say, six months or a year from now?

6. Have you ever had to correct someone's wrong understanding? What are the challenges in doing this effectively? Give an example of a time when you have seen this done well. Ask God to help you maintain a distinctively Christian character.

**Memory Verse**
2 Tim 2:15

*Do your best to present yourself to God as one approved, a workman who does not need to be ashamed and who correctly handles the word of truth.*

CHAPTER EIGHT

# CHOOSE
# WISE EXAMPLES

## 2 TIMOTHY 3:1-13

*"Example is not the main thing in influencing others. It is the only thing."*
—*Albert Schweitzer*

E thel sat beside her dying husband's bed. "Ethel," said Ray, "You've always been by my side. When we were poor newlyweds, you were there. When I broke my leg, you were there. When I lost my job in '72, you were there. When the fire destroyed our house in '87, you were there. Do you remember when I was in the car wreck? You were there. No matter what difficulty came our way, you were always there." Ray looked up at his wife with tears in his eyes, "You know something, Ethel? You're bad luck!"

Being around certain people is bad for you.

Someone said we have two kinds of relationships: balcony people and basement people. Balcony people lift us up—cheering us on and calling forth our best. Basement people, on the other hand, drag us down. They infect us with a negative attitude, discouraging us and leading us down the low road.

That's why Scripture is so clear that we are to guard our close associations. First Corinthians 15:33 says, "Do not be misled: Bad company corrupts good character." Motivational speaker Charlie "Tremendous" Jones once said, "You are the same today that you are going to be in five years except for two things: the people with whom you associate and the books you read." Paul would've agreed. Before telling Timothy to fill himself with the Good Book (3:14-17), the apostle tells him to surround himself with good people (3:1-13).

## Avoiding Dangerous Examples

Paul begins by warning Timothy of "basement people" in Ephesus that he should avoid. By the way, don't let the phrase "in the last days" fool you (3:1). That phrase is not pointing to some future era. In the New Testament, "the last days" began the moment Christ was born in Bethlehem. Both Acts 2:14-17 and Hebrews 1:1-2 make clear that "the last days" arrived with the first coming of Christ. The final era of history has begun. We are living in the last days, as was Timothy.

So the warning Paul gives here is not for the future, but for the present. In 3:1-9, Paul paints a picture of the false teachers that serves as a "wanted" poster. In fact, the word "terrible" in 3:1 could be translated "dangerous." It's used elsewhere to describe wild animals, wild seas, and wild human beings like the demon-possessed men in Matthew 8:28. The false teachers Paul will describe, then, are not just annoyances. They are threats. They pose a great danger to Timothy's spiritual health, as well as that of the Ephesian church.

The problem, of course, is that these false teachers can be hard to identify. They don't wear black hats or name tags that say, "Heretic." They don't stand up during Sunday morning announcements and say, "We're beginning a small group tonight where our teaching will lead you into the trap of the devil who will take you captive to do his will. You can sign up out in the church lobby on the clipboard marked 'False Teacher Fellowship Group.'"

Instead, these teachers appear very likable. They're knowledgeable, charismatic, and persuasive. In fact, they have already won the confidence of several women in the congregation (3:6). So how can Timothy distinguish genuine sheep from wolves in sheep's clothing (Matt 7:15)? The vice list in 3:2-4 acts as a police artist's sketch of the suspects. Timothy must keep his eyes open for those who match this description.

## Sketch of the Suspects

The vice list includes 19 character traits, and the first and last traits intentionally serve as bookends. The other 17 traits fall between, and are a result of, these two characteristics: "lovers of themselves . . . rather than lovers of God" (3:2,4). The proper order, of course, is to love God first, neighbor second, and self last. But these false teachers had switched first and third places. When we put self first and God last, our neighbor in the middle is bound to suffer. In fact, the other 17 vices listed are almost entirely about the false teachers' mistreatment of those around them.

As we study these vices, we ought to make two evaluations. First, evaluate yourself. Do you see these characteristics in your own life? All of us are capable of these vices, so look at this sketch, and then look in the mirror. We must guard our own hearts from the insidious increeping of sin.

Secondly, we ought to evaluate our close associations. Do you see these characteristics in your friends and influencers? Think also of your

media intake—TV, movies, music, Internet. Some people know their favorite sitcom characters better than they know their neighbors. Do these vices describe the musicians, bloggers, or movie characters you admire? The Bible clearly labels some people as evil. We are to avoid them, because they have fallen so deeply into sinful habits that they are now "men of depraved minds, who, as far as the faith is concerned, are rejected" (3:8). If we are not careful, these "basement people" will drag us down with them.

## Who's Your Role Model?

To help in these evaluations, I have summarized Paul's list of vices with six questions you can ask of your close associations.

- *Do they focus more on themselves or others?* Paul says they are "lovers of self," "boastful," and "proud." Pay attention to those who influence you: Do they show genuine interest in others or focus on themselves? In the 19th century, two of Britain's greatest politicians were William Gladstone and Benjamin Disraeli. It was said that when you dined with Gladstone, you thought you were *with* the world's most brilliant conversationalist. But when you dined with Disraeli—who could be equally as charming—he made you feel like *you* were the world's most brilliant conversationalist. Who are your friends more like—Gladstone or Disraeli?

- *Are they preoccupied with money or things?* Ephesus was an affluent city, the commercial center of Asia Minor. Money flowed like water. Like contemporary Americans, Timothy could easily have accommodated himself to a materialistic, consumer culture. Apparently the false teachers already had, because Paul calls them "lovers of money" and "lovers of pleasure." So ask yourself: are my role models focused on salary, house, car, clothes, boat, tech toys, stuff? Or do they live for more eternal interests?

- *How do they treat others—with kindness or rudeness/sarcasm?* Paul describes these men with words like "abusive," "disobedient to parents," and "slanderous." Do those around you speak against others unkindly? Do their attitudes reveal a callousness toward others' feelings? Do they speak disrespectfully to/about authority figures such as parents or a boss? Just as a doctor asks his patient to stick out her tongue and say "Ahhh," so we can check the spiritual health of those around us by paying attention to their tongue.

- *How would you describe their attitude—"entitled" or grateful?* The Roman philosopher Cicero said, "Gratitude is the mother of all virtues." When a person exhibits thankfulness, it evidences an appreciation of others' contributions, and that "others-awareness" can grow into kindness, patience, and other virtues. But the absence of gratitude signals a person who believes he has a right to the service others render. Other people exist for his benefit, and such self-centeredness can grow into the other vices Paul mentions here. That's why "ungrateful" is smack dab in the middle of the list.

- *Do they have a quick temper or act without thinking?* The false teachers are "without self-control" and "rash." These folks cannot control their impulses or their emotions. Proverbs 22:24-25 says, "Do not make friends with a hot-tempered man . . . or you may learn his ways."
- *Does their life show that they truly love God?* Do they speak of God, read His Word, pray, give their time or money to kingdom causes, obey scriptural commands, exhibit the fruit of the Spirit? If you have a hard time detecting these in the people you spend time with, they may fall under the labels "unholy" and "not lovers of God."

## Imitation Christianity

The bottom line is: these false teachers are hypocrites. Second Timothy 3:5 says they are displaying "a form of godliness but denying its power." They're all show and no substance, all talk and no walk, imitations and not the real thing. At an annual meeting of the American Heart Association, 300,000 doctors, nurses, and researchers met in Atlanta to discuss, among other things, the importance of a low fat diet. Yet during meal times, they ate foods like bacon cheeseburgers and fries at the same rate as people from other conventions. When one cardiologist was asked if his high fat meals set a bad example, he replied, "Not me, because I took my name tag off."

The false teachers had the same flawed thinking: as long as I say the right things, I don't have to do the right things. They were "always learning but never able to acknowledge the truth" (3:7). They read the Bible for information, but not for transformation. They may have known lots of biblical facts, but they didn't live biblically. If your leaders know ten times more Bible than anyone else but are zero times more joyful, loving, faithful, and self-controlled, watch out. Matthew Henry said, "Those who teach by their doctrine must teach by their life, or else they pull down with one hand what they build up with the other."

Paul knew the destructive influence the false teachers' example would have on their followers. As Proverbs 13:20 puts it, "He who walks with the wise grows wise, but a companion of fools suffers harm." The apostle did not want their lives to rub off on Timothy or the Ephesian church. Any vice can begin to spread like an infectious disease. So Paul gives Timothy one instruction about these bad examples: AVOID THEM.

> They're all show and no substance, all talk and no walk, imitations and not the real thing.

*Choose Wise Examples*

This does not mean Timothy is to treat them with a judgmental or superior attitude. Nor does it mean Timothy is to be an isolationist who avoids all contact with non-Christians. (How could we influence them for Christ?) First Corinthians 5:9-11 tells us to avoid immoral people in the church, not in the world.

Rather, Timothy is to avoid these false teachers to protect his own soul. He is to stay out from under their influence. Paul says they are like Jannes and Jambres, traditionally the names given to Pharaoh's magicians who opposed Moses (Exodus 7–9). These false teachers are imposters like those magicians were; they too stand in opposition to God, their judgment is coming, and Timothy won't want to be caught in the fallout.

We too must carefully evaluate who we allow to influence us. An ancient Greek proverb says, "A people are known by the heroes they crown." Who are our role models, our examples? Whose priorities, beliefs and habits tend to rub off on us? We must steadfastly avoid those who will lead us away from God. God will judge those whose faith is not genuine, and we don't want to be caught in the fallout.

Remember Ray and Ethel: being around certain people is bad for you.

## Choosing Wise Examples

On the other hand, being around certain people is good for you.

In verse 10, Paul turns from negative examples to a positive example—himself. While the apostle certainly knew his own sinfulness (1 Tim 1:15), he also pursued Christ so fervently that he often called others to follow in his footsteps (see 1 Thess 1:6; 2 Thess 3:7,9; 1 Cor 4:6; 11:1; Phil 3:17 and 4:9). If the false teachers were imitation Christianity, then Paul was Christianity worth imitating. His life was a kind of living Bible for others to read.

Timothy had clearly taken Paul as his role model. The word for "you know" in 3:10 is a strong Greek word, *parakolouthein*, which means "to follow physically, mentally, and spiritually." William Barclay writes, "*Parakolouthein* is indeed the word for the disciple, for it includes the unwavering loyalty of the true comrade, the understanding of the true student, and the obedience of the dedicated servant." Timothy had lived with, looked at, and learned from the great apostle.

In contrast to the false teachers, Paul offers a virtue list from his own life as a pattern for Timothy. Unlike the hypocritical teachers, Paul was the real deal. His conduct matched his creed, and he was the same man in the marketplace as in the church, in hard times as in good times. Paul reminds Timothy of things he's seen in Paul's life such as:

- *His purpose.* Paul lived for one thing alone: to know Christ and to make Him known (Phil 1:21).

- *His faith*. When it looked foolish to human eyes, Paul still trusted completely in God's promises.
- *His patience*. Timothy had watched as Paul refused to get irritated with frustrating people and circumstances. He kept his head.
- *His love*. Paul did not treat people as objects, projects, or a means to an end. He genuinely cared for them as a father does his children (1 Thess 2:11).
- *His endurance*. Certainly Timothy had witnessed the persecution the apostle had suffered. In fact, Timothy was from Lystra (3:11) where he may have seen Paul stoned and left for dead (Acts 14). Yet Paul wouldn't quit preaching the gospel.

Paul means for this list to stir Timothy's courage, to inspire him to follow the apostle's example. He wants Timothy to display the same virtues he saw in Paul's life, and Paul especially wants his own finish-line faith to rub off on Timothy. An ounce of example is worth a pound of preaching, so Paul points to his life and says, "If I can endure hunger, cold, loneliness, beating, flogging, stoning, and near death, you can surely endure the challenges of a difficult ministry."

> Paul especially wants his own finish-line faith to rub off on Timothy.

When New Testament scholar William Lane taught at Western Kentucky University, one of his students was contemporary Christian musician Michael Card. They developed a friendship that led to a discipling relationship, and Michael learned how to read Scripture, treat his wife, serve the church, and love God by watching Dr. Lane. Eventually Michael graduated, Dr. Lane moved to another university, and though they stayed in touch, their lives took separate paths.

Years later, Professor Lane was diagnosed with terminal cancer, and the Lanes decided to move to Franklin, Tennessee, where Michael Card lived with his family. As Card tells the story, Professor Lane had a purpose in this. He said to Michael on the phone, "I want to come to Franklin. . . . I want to show you how a Christian man dies." The Lanes made the move, and many months later Card's beloved mentor died. But he left behind a powerful lesson in finishing well.

That's what Paul has done for Timothy. Now Timothy must live what he has seen. Timothy will most certainly experience difficult times (3:12), but if he perseveres like Paul, the Lord will rescue him as well (3:11).

## The Power of a Positive Example

In applying this text to our lives, we ought to consider two questions. First, *do I have someone in whose footsteps I can follow?* Abraham Heschel wrote, "What we need more than anything else is not text-books but text-people. It is the personality of the teacher which is the text that the pupils read; the text they will never forget."

✤

C
H
A
P
T
E
R

8

*Choose Wise Examples*

Growing up, I watched my dad. I watched when he began every morning with his open Bible on his lap. I watched when he walked in the door every evening and his first order of business was kissing my mom. I watched when my corporate executive dad picked up the mentally handicapped guys from the county home for church and treated them with as much dignity as he would the company president. An African proverb says, "A good example is the tallest kind of preaching," and my dad's life is a sermon I'll never forget.

We all need those examples in our lives, so keep your eyes open. It may be a parent or grandparent, a leader in the church, someone in your small group or even someone whose life you've read about in church history. Don't put these people on a pedestal, but if they're truly following Christ, we can learn by following them.

The second question we ought to consider is this: *am I someone in whose footsteps others can follow?* We are called to live in such a way that we can say "follow my example as I follow the example of Christ" (1 Cor 11:1). Can you say to others: drive as I drive, spend money as I spend money, watch TV as I watch TV, love your spouse as I love my spouse, serve as I serve, speak as I speak, think as I think, walk as I walk?

If you want finish-line faith, choose wise examples. If you want those around you to have finish-line faith, be a wise example.

Remember Ray and Ethel? May you live in such a way that someday someone says: being around you was good for me. 3:16

# Going On When We Feel Like Giving In

1. Name some dangerous examples in our culture. What could the influence of people like this be? Have you ever seen a dangerous example in the church? What happened?

2. Look at the list of 6 evaluation questions in the chapter. Which one of these was most convicting to you personally?

3. Are there media influences in your life that you may need to reevaluate? Why do we sometimes enjoy these kinds of media (movies, TV, music, etc.) even when we know it's not helping our holiness? What could we replace it with?

4. Name some positive examples in your life. Whose life has been an inspiration or an influence?

5. Who is watching your example? To whom are you an influence? In what areas could you say, "Follow my example as I follow the example of Christ"? In what areas could you not say that?

6. Take time to thank God for the positive examples in your life. Ask Him for discernment and courage to make changes when we allow negative examples to influence us.

**Memory Verse**
2 Tim 3:12

*. . . everyone who wants to live a godly life in Christ Jesus will be persecuted. . . .*

# CHAPTER NINE

# NOURISH YOURSELF ON SCRIPTURE

## 2 TIMOTHY 3:14-17

*"A Bible that is falling apart usually belongs to someone whose life isn't."*
—*Charles Spurgeon*

You are what you eat.

Physically speaking, this dictum has some truth. If all you eat are carrots, you'll eventually be as skinny as a carrot. If all you ever eat are Big Macs, you'll eventually look like a Big Mac.

You are what you eat.

Spiritually speaking, this proverb rings even truer. What you feed your mind and soul will shape who you become.

True story: a young Austrian teenager wanted desperately to be an artist, but twice his application to the prestigious Vienna art school was sent back with the words "drawings unsatisfactory" scrawled across the top. Stung by the rejection, he did what many teenagers do—he withdrew into his own world. Isolated in his room, he devoured the writings of German philosopher Frederick Nietzsche who taught that God was dead and that the purpose of life was to gain power. He immersed himself in the music of Richard Wagner, whose anti-Semitism and rabid Germanic nationalism bled freely into his compositions. Of course, those books and that music profoundly shaped that young man . . . whose name was Adolf Hitler . . . and shaped the course of world history.

You are what you eat.

The music, television, books, magazines, conversations, movies, and Internet sites you constantly expose yourself to will mold your character. A Chinese proverb says, "Sow a thought; reap a deed. Sow a deed; reap a habit. Sow a habit; reap a character. Sow a character; reap a destiny."

Notice it all starts with a thought. "As a man thinks within himself, so is he" (Prov 23:7, KJV). What you put into your mind will determine who you become. You are what you eat.

That's why Scripture constantly uses the image of eating as a metaphor for Bible intake:

- "Then he said to me, 'Son of man, eat this scroll I am giving you and fill your stomach with it.' So I ate it, and it tasted as sweet as honey in my mouth" (Ezek 3:3).
- "How sweet are your words to my taste, sweeter than honey to my mouth" (Ps 119:103).
- "When your words came, I ate them; they were my joy and my heart's delight" (Jer 15:16)
- God's Word is compared to milk, bread, and meat (1 Pet 2:2; Deut 8:3; Heb 5:12).

We are to feed ourselves on the Word of Christ, so we can be transformed into the likeness of Christ. In 1 Timothy 4:6, Paul himself uses this metaphor with his young disciple. When he tells Timothy that a good minister of Christ Jesus is "brought up in the truths of the faith," the word for "brought up" literally means "nourished." Timothy is to nourish himself on Scripture.

Paul returns to this theme in 2 Timothy 3:14-17. As Timothy faces off against dangerous foes (3:1-9), he can draw strength from God's Word. The words of the Bible will get into his marrow, course through his veins, and metabolize into new energy, courage, and power. When he feels like giving up, God's Word will help give him finish-line faith.

## The Reasons for Scriptural Nourishment

Paul says that Timothy "from infancy has known the holy Scriptures." (This verse reminds us to start teaching the Bible even in the church nursery.) The Jewish people took the biblical education of their children seriously. One ancient Jewish rabbi said, "We take a child and stuff him with Torah [Old Testament Scriptures] like an ox." Starting at age 6, Jewish boys would start school at the village synagogue with the local rabbi.

Sometimes the rabbi would dip each child's fingers in honey—a rarity and the most enjoyable food they could imagine. Then the rabbi would say, "My child, lick the honey." As they did, he would remind them, "The Word of God is like honey. The Word of God is the most enjoyable thing you will ever taste." In each child's mind, Scripture was forever linked with pleasure, sweetness, and joy. While the half-Gentile Timothy might not have attended synagogue school, it is clear his Jewish mother and grandmother fed him generous helpings of God's Word from his earliest days.

But perhaps now he had lost his hunger for the truths of Scripture. We

✝

C
H
A
P
T
E
R

9

*Nourish Yourself on Scripture*

know that Paul tells Timothy not to abandon the Scriptures. "Continue in them," he says. "Abide in them, live in them, immerse yourself in them."

I read about an Ethiopian king named Menelik II who took the eating metaphor literally. Whenever he became sick, he would tear pages from the Bible and actually swallow them in the mistaken belief that this would cure him. He died in 1913 after devouring all of 2 Kings!

When I first read that story, I chuckled. Well, he took this eating imagery a little too seriously, didn't he? But then the Holy Spirit pricked my conscience: do I take this metaphor seriously enough? Jesus said, "Man does not live on bread alone, but on every word that comes from the mouth of God" (Matt 4:4). Is that true of me? Do I need God's Word to *live*?

Evaluate yourself. Would you feel hunger pangs if you went without reading your Bible? Can you truly say, as Job in 23:12, "I have treasured the words of His mouth more than my daily bread"?

Perhaps you have lost your hunger, and you too need to hear the reasons Paul gives Timothy to "continue" in the Scriptures (3:14).

## They're from God

Timothy must nourish himself on Scripture because they come to us straight from God. They are "God-breathed"—so fresh from His mouth you can still catch the scent of His breath on the pages. The Bible is like no other book. All other literature originates on this planet, but the Bible comes to us from outside our sphere of existence. It is literally from heaven.

I read about a little girl sitting next to her mother in church, looking over at her mother's open Bible. In a whisper, she asked, "Did God really write that?" "Yes," mom quietly whispered back. Looking down at the Bible again, the girl said in amazement, "Wow! He really has neat handwriting!"

Of course, God used human authors to write in their own distinctive handwriting. However, the unity of these authors—some 40 writers on three continents in three different languages over the course of 1500 years all telling the same story—points to Scripture's divine origin.

The humanity of these authors points to God's relational purpose. God stooped to speak to us through people like us—in understandable human language—so He could establish relationship with us. He could have remained above human contact, inscrutable, unreachable. But as Carl Henry said, the Bible is "God's free and gracious choice to give up His privacy that we may know Him."

In Scripture, God is allowing us to get inside His head, read His mail, eavesdrop on His heavenly council chamber, see the world through His eyes, and hear His most personal thoughts. Such behind-the-scenes access to the Creator of the Universe is nothing less than an invitation to *know* Him. Someone once said, "Books are the shoes with which we tread the footsteps of great minds." In the Bible we actually get to walk through the mind of God. Amazing! He must truly want a deep and intimate relationship with us.

This realization can stir a hunger for God's Word. Some time ago, my wife Katie and I were rummaging through an attic box of old college keepsakes. I reached for a large manila envelope, wondering what was inside. Old love letters! I pulled out a thick stack of envelopes Katie had sent me one summer when we were dating.

We were apart all summer, and I remember waiting eagerly for those twice-a-week letters in the mail. I would tear open the envelope and devour every sentence—reading and rereading every word, imagining the voice of my beloved speaking them to me. The letter read "Dear Matt," but behind the words I could hear her heart's true message—"my handsome hunk of a guy." Those letters were my lifeline to her. I didn't set out to memorize those letters, but I could almost quote them because I lingered over them so long.

(By the way, Katie pulled out of the manila envelope *both* of the letters I wrote her that summer. I'm a communications slob.)

Question: Why did I read these letters so hungrily? Because they were from someone I loved—someone who also loved me. Remember that the Bible is a personal letter to you from the Lover of your soul. He wrote it because He wants a relationship with you. We are to read this book because it is *from God*.

> Remember that the Bible is a personal letter to you from the Lover of your soul.

### They're about Christ

The Scriptures point to Jesus. That's the second reason Timothy is to nourish himself on God's Word. Paul reminds him that the Scriptures "are able to make you wise for salvation through faith in Christ Jesus" (3:15). Of course at this point, Timothy only had the Old Testament. But those 39 books were written to predict, prepare for, and describe the coming Messiah. In John 5:39 Jesus said, "The Scriptures . . . testify about me." In Luke 24:27 the resurrected Christ took the Emmaus travelers on a journey through the entire Bible, explaining to them "what was said in all the Scriptures concerning himself."

The Bible was written to reveal Christ. It is wonderfully diverse, but Jesus taught that all the stories and statutes, prophecies and proclamations, lists and laments, proverbs and prayers somehow found their focus in Him. If each section of Scripture is a puzzle piece, then when we put them together and step back, we see just one picture—or rather One Person. Norman Giesler put it this way:

- In the Law we find the foundation for Christ.

CHAPTER

- In the Books of History we find the preparation for Christ.
- In the Books of Poetry we find the aspiration for Christ.
- In the Prophets we find the expectation of Christ.
- In the Gospels we find the manifestation of Christ.
- In Acts we find the propagation of Christ.
- In the Epistles we find the interpretation of Christ.
- In Revelation we find the consummation in Christ.

So when someone wants to find Jesus, the best place to look is in the Bible. Martin Luther said, "Scripture is the manger in which Christ was laid."

As a Children's Church teacher, I am often asked to talk with children who are considering baptism. After attending church camp with a friend, a little girl named Tesslah decided she wanted to be baptized. I called her unchurched parents to ask if they would come to our church building on a Tuesday evening as I discussed baptism with their daughter. They agreed, listening in that evening as I explained to Tesslah what giving herself to Jesus meant.

They came the next Sunday when I baptized Tesslah, and I noticed that her mother Karen came back the following Sunday . . . and the following Sunday. After three weeks, she approached me on a Sunday morning with one of our church's free "take-one-if-you-want-one" Bibles in her hand. She said simply, "I've been reading this for three weeks, and I'm ready." In the pages of Scripture, she had come face to face with Jesus and wanted to follow Him.

Not only do the Scriptures lead us to initial faith in Jesus; after we become disciples, they continue to strengthen our faith in Him. Simply put, your soul's health is measured by this one test: how well do you know Christ? If He is your "Friend who sticks closer than a brother," your "Rock and Redeemer," the "Desire of your heart," then regardless of trials, you will find spiritual energy coursing through your veins.

But if you think little of Christ, are content to live without awareness of His presence, care little for His concerns, then you will find your soul weary and weak.

How then can you grow in your love and knowledge of Christ? Read His Word. St. Augustine said, "Ignorance of Scripture is ignorance of Christ." When you open the pages of Scripture, you will find yourself following along the dusty roads after the Galilean rabbi—hearing His voice, seeing His smile, watching His interactions with people like the ones you know, noticing the tiny moments of compassion that reveal His character, absorbing His passion for truth, listening to Him pray, and sharing in His life. He will walk off the pages and into the room where you are reading.

We are to nourish ourselves on the Scriptures because they are *about* Christ.

9  *Nourish Yourself on Scripture*

## They're for Us

What I mean is: they are for our good. The Scriptures teach us how to live "the life you've always wanted." Charles Spurgeon said it well, "A Bible that is falling apart usually belongs to someone whose life isn't." In 3:16, Paul tells Timothy that Scripture is useful for:

- Teaching: *telling us what's right.*
- Rebuking: *telling us what's not right.*
- Correcting: *telling us how to get right.*
- Training in Righteousness: *telling us how to stay right.*

Those who read the Bible regularly will find that, over time, their lives are being transformed. Bible reading is not like drinking caffeine—that instant jolt to get you through the next few hours. It's more like taking vitamins—strengthening you with greater health over the long haul. As you meditate on the words of Scripture, you will slowly become a person who is marked by goodness and joy and courage and patience and wisdom. When you pick up a Bible, you're not just holding 12 ounces of paper and ink and glue. You're holding the possibility of a whole new life.

Yet I wonder if more often we pick up the latest devotional book instead of our Bible. As a Bible college professor, I am often asked for book recommendations. Do I know of a good book on parenting/preaching/evangelism/marriage/money management? Understand: I am an avid book reader, and I'm grateful for every Max Lucado, Eugene Peterson, and Philip Yancey book on my shelf. But I always try to point people to Scripture first for the help they need.

- Want to sharpen your leadership? Read Nehemiah.
- Looking for money management advice? Read Proverbs.
- Exploring the meaning of life? Read Ecclesiastes.
- Dealing with a difficult boss? Read Daniel.
- Need to know how to romance your wife? Read Song of Songs.
- Want guidance on deepening your prayer life? Read Psalms.
- Trying to find joy in trials? Read Philippians.

You have an entire Christian bookstore between the covers of your Bible. Don't settle for good books without reading the best Book. Only God's Word is "living and active, sharper than any double-edged sword" (Heb 4:12). Only God's Word has the power to transform our lives. My friend Joe Puentes once told me that in his Hispanic community they have a saying, "Ha sido tan buena la Biblia con nosotros." *The Bible has been very good to us.*

> Don't settle for good books without reading the best Book.

We are to nourish ourselves on Scripture because it's from God, about Christ, and *for us.* If you fill your heart and mind with God's Word, it will be very good to you.

# The Strategies for Scriptural Nourishment

To close this chapter, may I suggest some practical application? How exactly can we take God's Word into our lives?

### Get It in Your Hand

Here I'm referring to regular Bible reading. In a Barna survey, over 80% of born-again Christians said they do not read the Bible daily. Almost 25% said they *never* read the Bible. We're facing what Amos 8:11 calls "a  famine of . . . the words of the LORD." Here in the United States, we have greater access to the Word of God than any people in history—available online, on CD, and in dozens of printed translations. The banqueting table is set, but we're starving ourselves.

So find a regular time that can be your standing appointment with God in His Word. Find a place that becomes your sanctuary, the Holy of Holies where you meet Him. Find a Bible reading plan that will help you read God's Word intelligently, systematically. Then make Bible reading a daily habit. As D.L. Moody put it, "A man can no more take in a supply of grace for the future than he can eat enough for the next six months. We must draw upon God's boundless store of grace from day to day."

So put down the remote control, the magazine, the iPod, the things that distract us, and pick up the knife and fork. A billboard sponsored by the cattlemen's association read, "Eat beef. The West wasn't won on salad." You won't develop finish-line faith by nibbling. Dive into the meat and potatoes of God's Word. Nourish yourself on Scripture.

### Get It in Your Heart

Here I'm referring to Bible meditation. Psalm 1:2 says the man of God "meditates day and night" on God's Word. While Eastern meditation seeks to *empty* the mind, biblical meditation seeks to *fill* the mind with God's truth. How? By giving time and reflection. Rather than gulping your Bible reading down and running on to your day's schedule, meditation chews Scripture slowly. This kind of reader "does not always remain bent over his pages; he often leans back and closes his eyes over a line he has been reading again" and its meaning enters his soul as food enters his stomach, spreads through his blood and becomes kindness and courage and wisdom and holiness.[1] This must be done slowly; you can speed read, but you cannot speed meditate.

What exactly does this meditation look like? Like a dog gnawing on a bone, turn the verse or phrase over and over in your mind, examining every word. Pray through it. Rewrite the text in your own words. Ask each word what it means. Warren Wiersbe says, "If you don't talk to your Bible, your Bible won't talk to you." So take time with a little piece of Scripture to converse with it, ask it questions. Savor every word, allowing all of its nutrients to soak into your mind and heart. Internalize it, because as Dallas Willard reminds us, "it is better in one year to have ten good verses transferred *into the substance of our lives* than to have every word of the Bible flash before our eyes."[2]

## Get It in Your Head

Here I'm referring to Bible memorization. The purpose of memorizing Scripture is to have it ready when the Holy Spirit needs it. The Holy Spirit wants to encourage us, shape us, teach us, mold us into the image of Christ, and the primary tools He uses are the truths of Scripture we've stored in our minds. But too often, He goes to our mental toolbox, and all He finds is a John 3:16. We haven't given Him much to work with.

Many people say they're bad at memorizing, but that's not true. It's a matter of motivation. If you can remember your Social Security number, your kids' names, and the words to "Jesus Loves Me," then you can memorize Scripture. The question is simply one of priority.

So pick one verse a week. Say it over and over. Meditate on it as described above. Write it on a 3×5 card and carry it with you. Pull it out when you have three minutes during the day to review. Stick it on your mirror as you get ready in the morning. Make it your computer screensaver. Practice writing it out from memory. Find a partner to memorize with.

As a missionary to China, J. Russell Morse was arrested in the 1940s for preaching Christ. He spent 15 months in a Chinese Communist prison. In telling the story of Morse, Seth Wilson wrote, "He endured severe tortures and terrific strain supported chiefly by his memory of the Bible. He testifies that the promises and precepts of God's Word came to him in memory and gave strength, wisdom and hope which were sorely needed. Therefore he urges all his brethren to fill their memories with that living and powerful Word."[3]

By the way, as Paul himself languishes in prison, he knows his own need to gather strength from Scripture. In 2 Timothy 4:13, he asks Timothy to come visit him quickly, bringing with him "the parchments." Most scholars agree: Paul is asking for his copies of the Old Testament Scriptures. He was arrested so suddenly that he wasn't able to grab his Bible, but now he wants to read it in his prison cell. After a lifetime of study (I'll bet Paul's Bible was well worn), he still wanted to read it again.

What a powerful example for Timothy to see! Paul finished well because he was, in John Wesley's words, "a man of one book." He had filled his life with God's Word, and in the process, he had become God's man.

Now Timothy must become such a man, so he must nourish himself on the Scriptures.

After all, you are what you eat. [3]

[1] Rainer Maria Rilke as quoted in Eugene Peterson, *Eat This Book* (Grand Rapids: Eerdmans, 2006) 4.

[2] Dallas Willard, *Hearing God: Developing a Conversational Relationship with God* (Downers Grove, IL: InterVarsity, 1999) 163.

[3] Seth Wilson, "Do You Have It in Your Heart?" *Learning from Jesus* (Joplin, MO: College Press, 1977) 22.

*Nourish Yourself on Scripture*

# Going On When We Feel Like Giving In

1. What's your favorite food? Donald Miller once wrote about a friend named Penny who told him, "We would eat chocolates . . . and read the Bible, which is the only way to do it, if you ask me. Don, the Bible is so good with chocolate. I always thought the Bible was more of a salad thing, you know, but it isn't. It is a chocolate thing." If the Bible was a food, what kind of food do you think it would be?

2. If the Bible is from God, what do you think He was trying to communicate to us? What is the big idea of the Bible? What was He trying to accomplish in writing it?

3. If the Bible is about Christ, in what ways does reading the Bible help us know Christ better? How has your Bible reading grown your relationship with Him?

4. The Bible was also written "for us"—to help us live a richer life. Name a time when learning biblical truths or principles helped you in a practical way. What is one of your favorite Bible verses or passages?

5. Rate your consistency in Bible intake on a scale of 1-10, with 1 being "never read it" and 10 being "every day." Do you ever meditate on or memorize Scripture? What has kept you from being as faithful as you'd like to be in Bible study?

6. Be sure to memorize this week's Bible verse. Thank God for the wonderful gift of His Word.

| Memory<br>Verse<br>2 Tim 3:16-17 | *All Scripture is God-breathed and is useful for teaching, rebuking, correcting and training in righteousness, [17]so that the man of God may be thoroughly equipped for every good work.* |
|---|---|

*Nourish Yourself on Scripture*

# CHAPTER TEN

# SPEAK GOD'S MESSAGE

## 2 TIMOTHY 4:1-8

*"Preach the gospel at all times. If necessary, use words."*
— St. Francis of Assisi

Some are noble. As the British prepared to hang Nathan Hale as a Revolutionary War spy, he uttered these famous words: "I only regret that I have but one life to give for my country."

Some are tender. On his deathbed, President James Polk whispered to his wife, "I love you, Sarah. For all eternity, I love you."

Some are despairing. As she lay dying, Queen Elizabeth the First wished for an impossible trade, "All my possessions for a moment of time."

Some are downright cranky. The final recorded words of author H.G. Wells were spoken to a nurse: "Go away! I'm all right."

Last words are many things, but the one thing last words are *not* is ignored. Shakespeare wrote, "The tongues of dying men enforce attention like deep harmony." When a man is on his deathbed, those around him lean in to listen well. We instinctively sense that final words are somehow important.

As Timothy nears the end of this letter, surely he knows he may be reading the apostle's last words. Timothy knows Paul is imprisoned in Rome on death row. Timothy knows that winter will soon shut down ocean travel, that he may not make it to Rome before Paul is executed. Timothy knows the parchment he holds in his hands may be his mentor's final letter.

I can see Timothy leaning in to listen to these last lines. He knows Paul will not waste his last breath; he will not spill his final ink carelessly. What beats most strongly in Paul's heart in this, his last hour? What charge does Paul most want to leave echoing in Timothy's mind?

> Last words are many things, but the one thing last words are not is ignored.

*In the presence of God and of Christ, who will judge the living and the dead, and in view of his appearing and his kingdom, I give you this charge: Preach the Word* (4:1).

## The Top Priority

Paul's last words are as simple as they are compelling: *Preach the Word.* The word "preach" simply means to "speak a message on behalf of the king." Paul is calling Timothy to speak God's message, to tell others about Christ. Timothy must give himself to the work of evangelism. Paul's last command is the same as Christ's in Matthew 28:19-20, "Go and make disciples of all nations, baptizing them . . . and teaching them."

By the way, this preaching is not restricted to those who occupy pulpits or draw salaries from a church. In Mark 1:45, the healed leper went about "preaching" the good news of what Jesus had done for him—the same word as in 2 Timothy 4:2. All of us who have experienced Jesus' healing touch are called to "preach."

*All of us who have experienced Jesus' healing touch are called to "preach."*

We have all been charged to spread the message of Jesus Christ to a waiting world. One lady was asked about her work. She replied, "I'm a missionary . . . cleverly disguised as a grocery store clerk." Every Christian is called to be a missionary, a preacher of the gospel. Jesus' last command is to be our first concern. Our top priority is to look for opportunities to tell the story of Jesus to those who have yet to follow Him.

St. Francis of Assisi said, "Preach the gospel at all times. If necessary, use words." Paul would've appreciated Francis's commitment to live his life as a sermon, but here Paul is saying, "Preach the gospel at all times. If *at all possible*, use words." In this text, Paul mentions three reasons why Timothy must speak God's message.

## Because Jesus Is Coming (4:1-2)

In 4:1, Paul mentions Christ's "appearing" when He "will judge the living and the dead." He is, of course, referring to Jesus' second coming. The Bible teaches that a day is coming when the trumpet of the archangel will sound, the eastern sky will split, and Jesus will come riding back to earth on the clouds, followed by His angel armies. History will end, time will cease, and all humanity will be judged—some to enjoy God's presence forever and others to eternal torment (Matt 24:27ff.; 25:31ff.).

The Bible describes Christ's return in at least two ways. First, it will be *unexpected*. First Thessalonians 5:1-2 says He will come like a thief in the night. No thief ever gave his victims a courtesy call as advance warning: "Hey, I just wanted to let you know I'll be robbing your house between

10:00–11:00 this evening. If you could leave the door unlocked and your TV unplugged, that would be great." Nor will we have any advance notice of Christ's return.

Second, Christ's return will be *soon*. In Revelation 22, the last chapter of the Bible, Jesus says three times, "I am coming soon" (7,12,20). All the prophecies to be fulfilled before His return have already taken place. There is nothing to prevent Jesus from crashing back through the clouds before you finish reading this sentence.

So if Jesus' return will be unexpected and soon, we must share the gospel with a sense of urgency. Who in your life still needs to hear about Christ? If you truly believe in heaven and hell, that person's eternal destiny hangs in the balance. Do not delay. Someone said, "If Satan cannot convince us that there is no heaven or hell, then he will convince us that there is no *hurry*." "You'll have opportunities later," he whispers. "There's no rush."

### A Proactive, Personal, Patient Witness

Paul, however, says differently. In verse 2, "be prepared" was a military word meaning "be on duty." The Message translates it: "Keep on your watch." We are to be vigilant in looking for opportunities to speak God's message. We are to speak "in season"—when it's convenient. We are to speak "out of season"—when it's not convenient.

In other words, we must *take* opportunities and *make* opportunities. John Stott writes, "We are given here not a biblical warrant for rudeness, but a biblical appeal against laziness."[1] If Jesus could return at any moment, then we must not grow lax in our responsibility as gospel messengers.

In speaking with others, however, we must be careful not to use a one-size-fits-all approach to evangelism. We must address each individual personally, tailoring our conversation to his or her unique needs:

- "Correct" and "rebuke" describe a *behavioral* approach. Some people are caught in sin and need to be confronted. They need you to speak to their *conscience*.
- "Encourage" describes an *emotional* approach. Some people are wounded by life and need to be strengthened. They need you to speak to their *heart*.
- "Careful instruction" describes an *intellectual* approach. Some people are troubled by doubts and need explanation. They need you to speak to their *mind*.

Paul adds that these spiritual conversations must be conducted "with great patience." When we care deeply about someone's spiritual destiny, we can get frustrated when they don't immediately embrace Christ as Lord. But conversion is a journey. Don't grow discouraged when someone doesn't instantly run all the way to the cross. Trust that each conversation can be a step in the right direction. Be patient.

But this patience is not the same as passivity. Paul's emphasis is that we must be proactive in our proclamation of Christ. I have a friend who keeps a sign on his office door with these two words: "Perhaps Today." So here's a question: If Jesus really could return today, what would you like Him to catch you doing?

Here's my favorite thought: I'd love for Jesus to catch me baptizing someone into Him. I'm standing in the baptistery with my friend, saying those familiar words as part of the ceremony: "Buried with Him in death and raised with Him in new life." Right when I say "raised," we actually start raising up out of the water and into the sky to meet Jesus! How cool would that be!

I once saw a bumper sticker that said, "Jesus is coming. Look busy." That's good advice. We ought to be busy in the work of evangelism. We must speak God's message because Jesus is coming soon to judge the living and the dead.

## An Irrecoverable Moment

In his autobiography *Just As I Am*, Billy Graham told of a golf outing with President Kennedy, a Catholic. Kennedy asked Mr. Graham if he believed in the Second Coming of Jesus Christ. When Billy said he most certainly did, Kennedy asked, "Well, does my church believe it?" Mr. Graham said it was in the Catholic Church's creeds, to which President Kennedy replied, "They don't preach it. They don't tell us much about it. I'd like to know what you think."

After Billy explained what the Bible said about Christ's return, Kennedy replied, "Very interesting. We'll have to talk more about that someday." Here is Billy's conclusion to the story:

> The last time I was with Kennedy was at the 1963 National Prayer Breakfast. I had the flu. After we both gave our talks, we walked out of the hotel to his car together. At the curb, he turned to me. "Billy, could you ride back to the White House with me? I'd like to talk with you for a minute."
>
> "Mr. President, I've got a fever," I protested. "I don't want to give you this thing. Couldn't we wait and talk some other time?" It was a cold, snowy day, and I was freezing as I stood there without my overcoat. "Of course," he said graciously.[2]

Then came November 22, 1963, and Billy Graham never saw President Kennedy alive again. Reflecting back, he writes, "His hesitation at the car door, and his request, haunt me still. What was on his mind? Should I have gone with him? It was an irrecoverable moment."[3]

The truth is: we do not know when our unsaved friends will stand before the judgment seat of Christ. That's why Paul writes elsewhere, "Be wise in the way you act toward outsiders; *make the most of every opportuni-*

*ty*" (Col 4:5). When you see a conversational opening to speak about spiritual matters, take it. You don't know if you'll get another chance. It may be an irrecoverable moment.

Jesus is coming, and eternity hangs in the balance. Preach the Word.

## Because Satan Is Deceiving (4:3-5)

A second reason Timothy is to speak God's message: he lives in a culture where truth is up for grabs. Paul says the people "turn their ears away from the truth and turn aside to myths" (4:4). The false teachers are saying whatever people want to hear. They are practicing "smorgasbord spirituality"—picking the truths they like and leaving the ones they don't.

Such smorgasbord spirituality is ultimately harmful for their hearers. When Paul says "men will not put up with sound doctrine," the word "sound" literally means *healthy* (4:3). As *The Message* translates this verse, "People will have no stomach for solid teaching, but will fill up on spiritual junk food." A diet of false teaching—no matter how pleasant it may be to hear—will leave them spiritually anemic. Of course, all of this is the work of the devil (1 Tim 4:1-2).

By the way, does any of this sound familiar? We too live in a culture where truth is up for grabs. No one truth can be imposed on others, our culture says. Everyone's beliefs are equally valid. The world's message is: to each his own. Your truth can conform to your taste—smorgasbord spirituality. Satan has convinced our culture that the only unforgivable sin is to believe in absolute truth.

### Keep On Speaking . . .

So how are we to respond to such a culture? In 4:5, Paul gives four instructions. First, *keep your head on straight.* Don't get deceived by false teachers yourself. The trouble with false teachers is that they smuggle 5% falsehood in a package of 95% truth, so listen carefully. Some of these teachers enjoy great popularity—with best-selling books, large churches, and national TV programs. If we don't keep our wits about us, we can find ourselves falling for "what itching ears want to hear."

Second, *expect hardship.* When we dare to speak the truth of Christ, we will not always be welcomed with open arms. When the apostles preached in the book of Acts, they got one of two responses—either a revival or a riot. We too should expect some hits when we speak God's message, but don't give up. We may cause a riot or two, but somewhere we might start a revival.

Third, *share the gospel as good news*. That's what Paul means by "the work of an evangelist." An "evangelist" in ancient times was a messenger who came with an announcement of good news—victory in battle, an imperial holiday, or the birth of a child. No one dreaded the words of an evangelist. They welcomed him with excitement and anticipation. His words were filled with joy.

Too often we act as if people will never want to hear what we have to say. Remember this: every human heart hungers for God. The false teachers may serve spiritual Twinkies and cotton candy, but a diet of junk food never satisfied anyone forever. We have the Bread of Life! We have what people really need. That's why someone described evangelism as "one beggar telling another beggar where to find bread." If the gospel is good news, then evangelism is transformed from a "have-to" to a "get-to." We get to share a truth that is liberating, satisfying, life-giving, and filled with joy. Don't treat the gospel like it's bad news.

Fourth, *don't give up*. Or as Paul puts it, "discharge all the duties of your ministry." Why? Because, while some will not welcome us with excitement and anticipation, *some will*. That's why we must keep preaching the Word. Some people will realize the emptiness in their soul is God-shaped. If we're not there to serve them "sound doctrine," who will? We are God's plan for sharing the good news. There is no Plan B. We must never stop making the Bread of Life available to a hungry world.

Satan is deceiving people, and only the truth can set them free. Preach the Word.

## Because Paul Is Leaving (4:6-8)

The final reason Timothy must speak God's message is simple but poignant: Paul won't be around to do it himself anymore. As Paul writes from the Mamertine Prison in Rome, he knows his time is short. In a few short weeks, the executioner's sword will fall. Paul uses several metaphors to describe his impending death.

- "Poured out like a drink offering" is a *sacrificial* metaphor, taken from Numbers 15:5-10. (See also Phil 2:17.) Paul says his life was a sacrifice, given in gratitude to God.
- Paul also uses a *nautical* metaphor. "Departure" pictures a boat loosing its moorings. Of Paul's many ocean voyages, he is ready now for his last, which will carry him safely to heaven's shore.
- "Fought the good fight" is a *military* metaphor. At the end of the day of battle, he stands exhausted—his sword arm heavy, his body fatigued, his strength spent. Others must carry on the fight in days ahead. But he knows his noble cause will ultimately be victorious, so he can leave the battlefield in peace.

- Paul then employs an *athletic* metaphor. He often compared the Christian life to a race (1 Cor 9:24-27; Gal 5:7; Phil 3:14). Now he says he has "finished the race" and will receive the victor's crown.

## The Baton Has Been Passed

The athletic imagery reminds me of my high school track experience. I ran the third leg of the 4×800 meter relay, and I vividly remember leaning forward at the starting line, palms sweating, heart beating out of my chest. I searched the pack of second-leg runners as they rounded the last curve, locked eyes with my teammate, and stuck out my hand. He slapped the baton into my palm, and I took off, running for all I was worth. Why did I run so hard? It was not just to achieve a personal best time. It was because I knew my teammates who had run before me were counting on me.

Paul here is saying to Timothy, "I have finished my leg of the race, and now I'm passing the baton to you, Timothy. I'm counting on you to continue my work, so run hard and hold on tight." He is leaving, so now Timothy must take over. Paul is depending on him to preach, teach, evangelize, correct, and encourage just as the apostle did. As Joshua followed Moses, as Elisha followed Elijah, so Timothy must follow Paul.

Here's a question: who passed the baton to you? You didn't get into the kingdom on your own. Someone spoke God's message to you—maybe a friend, your parents, a minister, a grandparent, or a coworker. Someone 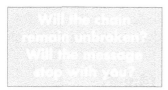 told them about Jesus, and then they told you. The question is: will the chain remain unbroken? Will you in turn tell someone else about Jesus, or will the message stop with you? The baton has been passed, and now you must continue someone else's ministry.

## Who Will Fill His Shoes?

When I was a Bible college student, I accepted a part-time youth ministry at a church in town. The preacher, Bob Ely, quickly became a trusted mentor. Bob was the definition of high energy, a dirt bike racer and a biplane pilot. He never walked; he just sorta bounced from one place to another, with a mischievous sparkle in his eye and a smile underneath his mustache.

One of my first memories of Bob: I'd only been working at the church for a week, and Valentine's Day was Friday. I couldn't afford to take my fiancée Katie to a nice restaurant, so I asked Bob if I could use the church office that night. He said yes, so I set up a card table with a red tablecloth and candle. I could afford a half gallon of ice cream, so I dipped out two Styrofoam plates of ice cream, sculpted it into heart shapes, lined them with Red Hots and put them in the freezer. (Sappy? Yes, but cheap.)

That evening, I took Katie out to the darkened church and surprised her. As we sat there eating our ice cream by candlelight, guess who appeared at the office door with guitar in hand? Bob never said a word. He just smiled, serenaded us with two love songs, and then disappeared into the night. It was hard not to like Bob.

He was a solid preacher. I remember one sermon he preached from Deuteronomy 31. He placed a pair of sandals on the modesty rail by the pulpit and talked about Joshua filling Moses' sandals, succeeding him as leader. Then Bob placed a pair of black dress shoes by the sandals and talked about John Martin, a longtime faithful elder who had recently passed away. He asked, "Who will fill John Martin's shoes?"

It was a good sermon, but Bob did his best preaching one-on-one. He'd grab me and say, "Come on, Proctor. Let's go talk to some people about Jesus." We'd hop in his red Mazda pickup, go to the Dairy Queen not far from the church, and talk to the ladies behind the counter about Jesus. We went to living rooms, hospital rooms, the bleachers at kids' ballgames and talked with people about Jesus.

Bob kept a pair of muddy work boots in the back of his truck. He'd drive up Highway 43 to Chism's farm, throw on his boots, and work out in the field alongside Jay Chism, talking about Jesus. Jay and Mindy Chism still attend that church. Bob preached his best sermons in farm fields, on front porch swings, and over restaurant counters, and I was there watching, listening, and learning.

I graduated from Bible college and became the preacher of a little church in Carbondale, Illinois. I'd only been there nine months when I got a phone call telling me Bob's biplane had crashed. He was killed instantly.

Katie and I drove back to Missouri for his funeral. That little church of 150 where I'd been the youth minister was crowded with over 300 people—lives that Bob had touched. As I sat in the pew listening to the funeral message, I couldn't help but imagine, up on the modesty rail by the pulpit, a pair of muddy work boots.

Who would take Bob's place? Who would fill his shoes?

I drove back to my ministry in Illinois. I helped a farm family put up hay, went to kids' ballgames, sat in living rooms and hospital rooms and on front porch swings. I visited the Dairy Queen three blocks from our church. And everywhere I went, I tried to talk about Jesus. I can't help but think: somehow Bob's ministry lived on in me.

Whose ministry lives on in you? Someone passed you the baton. Don't drop it. Tell someone else about Jesus. Speak God's message. Take the apostle Paul's last words as a personal charge to you.

Preach the Word. 3:16

---

[1] Stott, *Message of 2 Timothy*, 107.
[2] Billy Graham, *Just As I Am* (San Francisco: Harper-Collins, 1997) 472-473.
[3] Ibid., 473.

# Going On When We Feel Like Giving In

1. What would you like your last words to be? What do you think you would be thinking about in your last moments? How does that compare to what Paul was thinking about?

2. Who in your sphere of influence needs to know about Christ? Do you see yourself as a missionary to those around you? What might change in your behavior if you saw yourself this way?

3. How often do you think about the imminent return of Jesus? What are ways you could remind yourself about the urgency of time?

4. The verbs in 4:2 each describe a different approach to speaking with people. Think of the person you want to reach. What approach might be most effective? Why? What are specific ways that you could make an opportunity to speak with them?

5. Have you ever gotten discouraged in your efforts to witness to someone? What could help you not lose heart?

6. Who is it that passed you the baton—who told you about Jesus? Take time right now to thank God for their willingness, patience, and courage. Ask Him to give you open conversational doors, the right words, and the courage to tell someone else the good news.

**Memory Verse** 2 Tim 4:5

*But you, keep your head in all situations, endure hardship, do the work of an evangelist, discharge all the duties of your ministry.*

# CHAPTER ELEVEN

# CULTIVATE REAL COMMUNITY

## 2 TIMOTHY 4:9-15,19-22

*"Call it a clan, call it a tribe, call it a network, call it a family.
Whatever you call it, whoever you are, you need one."*
—Jane Howard

Several years ago, two of my nephews accompanied their mom on a visit to a friend's house. Ben was 8, Brian was 6. Their mother's friend was a very neat lady—a place for everything and everything in its place. She had defeated clutter and driven it from her home. Though childless, she did have a few toys and handed Ben and Brian a bucket of Legos: "Here, boys, you can play with these."

What's the first thing they did with that bucket? Like all red-blooded American boys, they dumped it out. Their mother's uptight friend immediately went into full obsessive-compulsive mode. She dropped to her knees and started scooping the Lego pieces back into the bucket with these words: "No, no, no, boys. What I meant was, you can play with these . . . one at a time."

What?

You might be able to play with dolls or Hot Wheels cars one at a time, but *you can't play with Legos one at time!* A Lego piece's whole purpose is to be combined with other pieces. A Lego piece is created to be part of a group, something bigger than itself. A solitary Lego can never fulfill its destiny. Legos were made to be connected.

## Lego Theology

You don't have to read far into your Bible to discover: human beings were created to be combined with other human beings.

Human beings were created to be combined with other human beings.

99

In Genesis 1, God makes the world and declares, "It is good." But after creating a man, God says, "It is not good." Why? Because the man is alone. There's only one of him, and humans aren't meant to do life one at a time. So God decides to split the Adam. (I know, bad joke.) He makes Eve from Adam's rib to be his life-partner, and only then can God say, "It is very good." Call it Lego theology: human beings were made to be connected. We were created for community.

That's because we are created in God's image (Gen 1:27). God, of course, is a Trinity—completely One, yet in Three Persons. From eternity past, the Father, the Son, and the Spirit have lived together in perfect community. Professor Oscar Thompson used to say the most important word in the English language was the word *relationship*. He might be right, because God is all about relationship. Since before the beginning of time, the Father, the Son, and the Spirit have enjoyed each other, served each other, valued each other, understood each other, and loved each other. At the center of the universe lives a Divine Community, Three Persons who are inseparably and wonderfully *connected*.

As humans created in God's image, we too are made for relationship. A solitary human being can never fulfill his destiny. You will never finish well on your own—literally. A landmark Harvard study of 7,000 people found that the most isolated people were *three times more likely to die* than those with strong relationships. Reporting on the study, John Ortberg writes that "people who had bad health habits (such as smoking, poor eat-

 ing habits, or alcohol use) but strong social ties lived *significantly longer* than people who had great health habits but were isolated. In other words, it is better to eat Twinkies with good friends than to eat broccoli alone."[1]

What is true physically is also true spiritually: we need community. That's why God invented the church. The Christian life is meant to be a life lived together. Too many in our culture say they're committed to Jesus, but not the church. Disillusioned with imperfect churches, they take a "just-me-and-Jesus" approach.

But not even Jesus did that. He didn't take a "just-Me-and- . . . Me" approach. He gathered a very imperfect community of twelve to share life with. Jesus didn't begin the Lord's Prayer, "*My* Father who art in heaven." He taught us to pray "*Our* Father." While the gospel is certainly personal, it is never individual. If you belong to Jesus, you also belong to everyone else who belongs to Jesus. Imperfect as it is, the church is part of the package.

## Don't Skip the Final Paragraphs

The apostle Paul knew this deep in his bones. Too often, we picture Paul as the great solo missionary, a lone evangelist heroically moving from one church plant to the next. That may be because, as Bible readers, we instinctively skip the closing sections of his letters. The NIV paragraph headings usually read "Personal Remarks" or "Final Greetings." No real substance there, right? Paul's already finished his doctrinal and ethical teaching. The sermon's over, and the final paragraphs are mostly like the post-worship-service conversations out in the church lobby—a bunch of greetings that are nice, but not important.

Not true. These final paragraphs teach us something immensely important: Paul never did life alone. Read Romans 16, 1 Corinthians 16, or Colossians 4, and you'll find dozens of names, names of those Paul constantly leaned on for encouragement, partnership, and wisdom. Paul was wary of what someone called "the peril of the solitary life." So he intentionally gathered around him a "band of brothers," a little community of faith to uphold him. He stayed connected.

Yet here in prison in 2 Timothy 4, for a number of reasons, Paul feels almost completely isolated in prison, cut off from those close to him:

> He intentionally gathered around him a "band of brothers."

- Demas deserted him because "he loved this world" (4:10). Was it fleshly temptation or simply fear for his own life that pulled Demas from Paul's side? This close associate's abandonment—elsewhere Paul calls him a "fellow worker"—must have pained the apostle deeply (Phmn 24).
- Crescens and Titus have traveled to Galatia and Dalmatia, respectively (4:10). Since Paul doesn't censure his coworkers, they are presumably on legitimate kingdom business, but they're absent nonetheless.
- Tychicus is on his way to Ephesus with the letter of 2 Timothy in hand (4:12).
- After Paul's arrest, Erastus and Trophimus had apparently been traveling with Paul to Rome (4:20). But when they arrived in Corinth, Erastus left the apostle to stay in his hometown (Rom 16:23). Trophimus made it as far as Miletus before succumbing to illness.
- Only Luke, the faithful doctor, is still at Paul's side (4:11). Can you picture these two old men sitting together in the Roman prison cell? Balding but for a few wisps of gray hair, ragged clothes, shivering when temperatures drop at night?

Paul is lonely, so as he closes the letter, he urges Timothy to get Mark and come visit him in Rome. Winter is coming when the seas are closed to traffic—from November through February. If Timothy waits until spring, he may end up visiting Paul's grave instead of Paul's prison cell. So he says, "Come before winter" (v. 21).

He asks Timothy to stop in Troas—which may be where Paul was arrested—to gather a few things left there. (While there, Timothy must be on guard against Alexander. The verb "did me great harm" literally means "to inform against" [v. 14]. Was Alexander the informer responsible for Paul's arrest?) Paul wants his books, especially his Bible, for the sake of his mind. He wants his cloak for the sake of his body. But most of all, he wants the companionship of Timothy and Mark for the sake of his soul.

## The Multiplication of Courage

Though Nelson Mandela was imprisoned for 27 years, he emerged to lead South Africa out of apartheid. His relationships with his fellow political prisoners sustained him through years of intense suffering. In his autobiography, he wrote:

> It would be very hard if not impossible for one man alone to resist. But the authorities' greatest mistake was to keep us together, for together our determination was reinforced. We supported each other and gained strength from each other. Whatever we learned, we shared, and by sharing we multiplied whatever courage we had individually. The stronger ones raised up the weaker ones, and both became stronger in the process.[2]

Paul knows that, in community, his courage will be multiplied, so he pleads with Timothy to come quickly. But the wise apostle is surely seeking to multiply Timothy's courage as well. He wants to model for "timid Timothy" the strength found in real Christian fellowship.

By the way, fellowship in Scripture (the Greek word *koinonia*) is more than church potluck dinners. Too often we sit in the church fellowship hall, eat casserole, talk about the weather, the football game, and our truck's gas mileage, and then leave with the farewell: "Nice fellowshipping with you, Ray." This is Christian *socializing*, which can be a great joy.

But the difference between Christian socializing and Christian fellowship is the difference between eating a donut and eating a square meal—one is fun, but the other is necessary for real health. True Christian *koinonia* happens when we get past surface conversation, crack the door on our hearts, and share our spiritual life together.

When community happens, we talk about what we don't understand about the Bible, what God is teaching us as we read, where we're struggling, who we're serving, who's frustrating us, what decisions we face, and what blessings we're experiencing. We encourage, admonish, comfort, challenge, serve, rejoice with, mourn with, submit to, forgive, share with, bear with, care for, and pray for one another. That's *koinonia*, and when that is cultivated, our courage to persevere through tough times is multiplied. By mentioning the names in this section, Paul suggests at least three things Timothy can find in real Christian community.

## A Warm Welcome

As you reflect on the names in 2 Timothy 4, their diversity is striking. This is not a homogenous group of people. You find differences in:

- *Occupation.* Luke is a doctor (Col 4:14). Erastus is a politician (Rom 16:13). Priscilla and Aquila are tentmakers (Acts 18:2-3).
- *Age.* Timothy and Mark are both younger thirty-somethings. Paul and Luke are likely both in their sixties.
- *Gender.* Some Jewish rabbis viewed women as second-class citizens, daily praying, "Thank you, God, for not making me a Gentile, slave or woman." Paul, however, speaks of Priscilla and Claudia as valued fellow-believers.
- *Race.* Paul and Mark are Jewish. Titus and Luke are Greeks. Timothy is half-Jewish, half Greek. Pudens and Linus are Roman.

Despite these differences, however, they are family. Paul's favorite term for Christ-followers—more than "saints," "Christians," "believers"—is "brothers." In his letters, he refers to fellow believers over sixty times as "brothers," including here in our text (4:21). Amazingly, in a world where prejudices run high, each person in this markedly diverse list has been given a warm welcome into the family of God. They have taken to heart Paul's words in Romans 15:7, "Accept one another, then, just as Christ accepted you."

When I served as a preacher in Carbondale, Illinois, I became friends with a young man in my congregation named Aminu Timberlake. Aminu played basketball for Southern Illinois University, and through his room-mate's witness, he became a Christian and joined our church. He came to me with questions about the Bible. We talked often and enjoyed joking around together. I performed his wedding. So when I was preparing to leave that ministry, Aminu made sure to stop by to say his good-byes. He gave me a big bear hug with these words, "You and me—we've got to stay in touch, because you and me—we're like family."

To anyone eavesdropping at that moment, those would've been strange words. Aminu is black; I'm white. Aminu is 6'9" tall; I'm 5'9" tall. Aminu grew up in a tough neighborhood on the South Side of Chicago; I grew up in Iowa. Aminu was from a family of lifelong Democrats; my dad's initials (honest truth) are GOP. Aminu was Big Man On Campus, a starter for a Division I basketball program; I was the unknown preacher of a little church on the west side of town. You probably couldn't have found two guys more different.

Family? Absolutely. As Bob Russell says, "A man doesn't have to be my twin to be my brother." In the community of Christ, despite our differences, we welcome each other as He welcomed us. Paul wants Timothy to stay connected because, though the world may reject him, he will always find a warm welcome in the family of God.

C
H
A
P
T
E
R

## A Second Chance

When you're different from others, the offer of a warm welcome is a kindness; but when you're disappointing to others, the offer of a second chance is nothing short of a marvel. That's because the law of this world is justice, not grace. You've heard the words used when one person has betrayed another: "She'll get what's coming to her," "He'll reap what he's sown," "What goes around comes around." The default human setting is not forgiveness; it's revenge. Second chances aren't our first instinct.

But things are different in the community of faith. Take Mark, for example. He accompanied Paul and his cousin Barnabas on the apostle's first missionary journey, but deserts them before the journey is over (Acts 13:13). Was he homesick, afraid of bandits, or intimidated by the stiff climb over the Taurus mountains? We don't know. But we do know that, when Barnabas suggests taking Mark along on their second missionary journey, Paul's disappointment ran so deep that he split up with Barnabas rather than travel again with Mark (Acts 15:38-39). At that point, Paul wasn't ready to give a second chance.

Ever felt like that? I heard of a guy who dialed a friend's phone number and got this message: "I am not available right now, but thank you for caring enough to call. I am making some changes in my life. Please leave a message after the beep. If I do not return your call, you are one of the changes."

The fact is: sometimes we wish we could just delete difficult people from our lives. The Bible is very honest about the challenges of living in

community. The New Testament does not paint a picture of the church as people who live together in perpetual smileyhood and niceness. Community gets messy, and that's why there are Scriptural admonitions like:

- Be patient with one another (implied: "because people will annoy you.")
- Bear with one another (implied: "because people will aggravate you.")
- Forgive one another (implied: "because people will hurt you.")

When someone disappoints us, we are tempted to wash our hands of him. I heard of a young lady breaking up with her boyfriend who said, "I will always cherish the initial misconception I had about you." Ouch. But Dietrich Bonhoeffer wrote that true community *begins* with disappointment. Real *koinonia* begins when we painfully realize that someone isn't perfect and we choose to love them anyway. We can't love people for who we wish they were. We can only love them for who they actually are.

So we forgive and go on. Forgiveness doesn't mean that we fail to deal with the conflict. Someone said there is a difference between peace*making* and peace*faking*—one works through difficulties while the other ignores them. Forgiving is not just forgetting—acting like nothing happened.

Instead, forgiveness involves releasing your anger and seeking to reconnect in appropriate ways. We refuse to turn our back on the one who hurt us. As Ken Idleman once put it, "Godly leaders have no disposable relationships."

Eventually, Paul realized this. Somewhere along the way, he forgave Mark and offered him a second chance. Now he wants to see Mark before he dies and calls him "helpful to me in my ministry" (4:11). That's the beauty of Christian community: our failures are not fatal. We receive grace, and Paul wants Timothy to stay connected because only in the church will he find a second chance.

> That's the beauty of Christian community: our failures are not fatal.

## A Helping Hand

Finally, Paul knows Timothy will find in Christian fellowship a helping hand when he needs it. Paul had. He mentions Priscilla and Aquila who at some point, he says in Romans 16:4, "risked their lives for me." The Greek could literally be translated "stuck their necks out for me"—a figure of speech not to be taken lightly in an age when the executioner's axe was not a metaphor. Somehow this courageous couple had placed themselves in great peril to help their friend Paul.

Paul also references Onesiphorus, whose name means "profitable" and who was mentioned earlier in the letter (1:16-18; 4:19). There he said Onesiphorus came to Rome from Ephesus and searched hard for the aged prisoner, likely taking his life in his hands to do so. Paul says that Onesiphorus "often refreshed" him and, earlier in Ephesus, had "helped" him in many ways (1:16,18). That's at the very core of true Christian community. We help each other. Whether it's financial assistance, a listening ear, lawn mowing, babysitting, a car to borrow, advice on parenting, a shoulder to cry on, or a place to stay, we do what we can to meet each other's needs. One of the most amazing statements made of the early church is that, because of the many helping hands, "there were no needy persons among them" (Acts 4:34).

Pastor Stu Weber paints a picture of such a helping community with a story from his days in Army Ranger training:

> We'd been running every day, but this was something else. This was the physical training stage of U.S. Army Ranger School, and we expected exertion, even exhaustion. But this was no morning PT rah-rah run in T-shirts. We ran in full field uniform. Loaded packs. Helmets. Boots. Rifles. As usual, the word was, "You go out together, you stick together, and you come in together. If you don't come in together, don't bother to come in!"
>
> Somewhere along the way, I noticed one of the guys was out of sync: a big, rawboned redhead named Sanderson. His legs were pump-

C
H
A
P
T
E
R

ing, but he was out of step with the rest of us. Then his head began to loll from side to side. This guy was struggling—close to losing it.

Without missing a step, the Ranger on Sanderson's right reached over and took the distressed man's rifle. Now one of the Rangers was packing two weapons—his own and Sanderson's. The big redhead did better for a time. But then while the platoon kept moving, his jaw became slack, his eyes glazed, and soon he began to sway again. This time, the ranger on his left reached over, removed Sanderson's helmet, tucked it under his own arm, and continued to run. All systems go. Our boots thudded along the dirt trail in heavy unison. Tromp-tromp-tromp-tromp!

Sanderson was hurting, really hurting. He was buckling, going down. But no, two soldiers behind him lifted the pack off his back, each taking a shoulder strap in his free hand. Sanderson gathered his remaining strength, squared his shoulders, and the platoon continued to run—all the way to the finish line. We left together. We returned together. And all of us were the stronger for it.

Together is better.[3]

So don't skip the final paragraphs of this letter. In this list of names, Paul's message to Timothy is powerful: beware "the peril of the solitary life." Don't try to go it alone. If you want to cross the finish line of faith, stay connected. Together with other believers, you will find a warm welcome. Together with other believers, you will find a second chance. Together with other believers, you will find a helping hand.

Together is better. 🔲

---

[1] John Ortberg, *Everybody's Normal Till You Get to Know Them* (Grand Rapids: Zondervan, 2003) 33.

[2] Nelson Mandela, *Long Walk to Freedom* (Austin, TX: Holt/McDougal, 2000) 390.

[3] Stu Weber, *Locking Arms* (Sisters, OR: Multnomah, 1995) 13-14.

✝

C
H
A
P
T
E
R

11  *Cultivate Real Community*

# Going On When We Feel Like Giving In

1. An introvert is not necessarily shy, nor is an extrovert necessarily super outgoing. Rather, the difference between an introvert and extrovert is this: extroverts recharge their emotional batteries by being around people; introverts recharge by getting alone time. Are you an introvert or an extrovert? On a scale of 1-10, how relational are you?

2. Do you know people who say they are Christians but have nothing to do with the church? How does that square with what we see of Christians in the New Testament? Why do you think some people who say they love Jesus still avoid the church? What are some of the "perils of the solitary life"?

3. Remember the distinction between Christian socializing and Christian fellowship. We need both. How much of the first do you think do? How much of the second do you think you experience? Who is your "band of brothers" that you do life with?

4. How well does your congregation do at extending a "warm welcome" to those who are different? How diverse is your church? Why do you think that is? How well do you personally do at giving a warm welcome? What could you do to improve?

5. "True community *begins* with disappointment—when we realize someone isn't perfect and choose to love them anyway." Have you ever had to deal with someone who hurt or disappointed you? How did you handle it? What does it take to forgive and give a second chance?

6. Is there someone in your church right now who needs a helping hand? What practical thing could you or your small group do this next week to help?

7. Take time to thank God for the gift of the Christian community. Ask Him to give you patience when people are disappointing. Thank Him that others are patient when you're disappointing.

*All the believers were one in heart and mind. No one claimed that any of his possessions was his own, but they shared everything they had. [33]With great power the apostles continued to testify to the resurrection of the Lord Jesus, and much grace was upon them all. [34]There were no needy persons among them. For from time to time those who owned lands or houses sold them, brought the money from the sales [35]and put it at the apostles' feet, and it was distributed to anyone as he had need.*

# Conclusion

# Stay Close to Jesus

**2 TIMOTHY 4:16-18**

*"Peace is not the absence of affliction, but the presence of God."*
*—Anonymous*

A mother washing dishes after dinner asked her little boy to go out on the back porch to get the broom. Out of the corner of her eye, she watched five-year-old Johnny go to the back door, open it, and look out for a few moments before returning to sit at the kitchen table. Sensing what was wrong, she sat down at the table. "You're scared of the dark, aren't you Johnny?" she asked. He nodded his head.

His mother smiled reassuringly, "You don't have to be afraid, honey. Remember: Jesus is always with you. That means He's right out there on that back porch too, so you don't have to be afraid. Okay?"

"Okay, Mama," said little Johnny. His mother went back to her dishes and watched again as Johnny went to the back door. He cracked it open, poked his head out, but didn't step out. "Jesus, I know you're right out here on this back porch with me," she heard him say. "So do you mind handing me that broom over there?"

When you face difficult times, the presence of Christ makes all the difference.

In our study of 2 Timothy, we've looked at several ways to develop finish-line faith. But in this race called the Christian life, the most important thing is this: *stay close to Jesus.* When the writer of Hebrews wrote, "Let us run with perseverance the race marked out for us," he followed it immediately with, "Let us fix our eyes on Jesus" (Heb 12:1-2). That's because:

- When we are afraid, Jesus gives us courage.
- When we are weary, Jesus gives us strength.
- When we are confused, Jesus gives us guidance.

109

- When we are grieving, Jesus gives us comfort.
- When we are guilty, Jesus gives us grace.

Second Timothy 2:1 is a pivotal verse in this letter. Paul tells Timothy, "You then, my son, be strong in the grace that is in Christ Jesus." Paul is wise. Telling Timothy to be strong in and of himself would have been "futile, even absurd. He might as well have told a snail to be quick or a horse to fly as command a man as timid as Timothy to be strong."[1]

But Paul isn't telling Timothy to be strong in himself. Timothy is to find his strength *in Christ*. In fact, "be strong" is a passive verb—literally, "be strengthened." This is not something Timothy does; rather it is something

 that is done to Timothy. In John 15:5, Jesus said, "I am the vine; you are the branches. If a man remains in me and I in him, he will bear much fruit; apart from me you can do nothing." Timothy's job is simply to remain in Jesus; Jesus' job is to give him the strength to cross the finish line.

## Paul Finishes with a Testimony

Paul knows this better than anyone. For over 30 years, he has leaned on Jesus. He is painfully aware of his own limitations—spiritually, emotionally, physically; he knows he cannot do it on his own. So the apostle counts on the great promise the Lord made to him: "My grace is sufficient for you, for my power is made perfect in weakness" (2 Cor 12:9). In fact, he says, "Therefore I will boast all the more gladly about my weaknesses, so that Christ's power may rest on me. That is why, for Christ's sake, I delight in weaknesses, in insults, in hardships, in persecutions, in difficulties. For when I am weak, then I am strong" (2 Cor 12:9-10).

Nowhere do we see this more clearly than in 2 Timothy 4:16-18. These are the last of Paul's last words, the final words of his final recorded letter. In the closing camera shot before the end credits roll, we see Paul in his Roman prison cell, reflecting on Christ's faithful presence.

Jesus had promised that He would never leave or forsake His own, that He would be with them "always, to the very end of the age" (Matt 28:20). Paul is testifying that Jesus has kept His promise.

Paul says in 4:16-17, "At my first defense, no one came to my support, but everyone deserted me . . . but the Lord stood at my side and gave me strength." In a Roman trial, an initial hearing was held to determine if a full-blown trial was needed, and Paul says none of his friends stepped forward at this hearing to act as his advocates or witnesses. Yet he sensed Christ beside him, strengthening him (Phil 4:13).

In fact, Jesus gave Paul the boldness to seize this moment to proclaim the gospel so that "all the Gentiles might hear it." John Stott paints the pic-

CONCLUSION

ture: "In one of the highest tribunals of the empire, before his judges and perhaps before the emperor himself, no doubt with a large crowd of the general public present, Paul 'preached the word.'"[2] Instead of pleading his own case at his hearing, Paul grabs the moment to plead the case of Christ. That's finishing strong!

Paul's testimony goes on: "And I was delivered from the lion's mouth" (4:17). Paul was spared immediate death, he says, because Christ delivered him just as He had delivered Daniel in the Old Testament. Back then, Daniel appeared powerless but was never at any moment out of the safekeeping of his God. As William Augustus once wrote, "Daniel was not in the lion's den. The lions were in Daniel's den." So too, the apostle is confident that Jesus, not the emperor, is in complete control of his situation.

Paul is finishing well—still preaching, still praying, still encouraging, still trusting—for one simple reason: he is close to Jesus, and he knows Jesus is close to him. The fact is: we are often closest to Christ when the times are toughest. Think about this biblically:

- It is only in the fiery furnace that Shadrach, Meshach, and Abednego get to walk side by side with one "like a son of god" (Dan 3:25).
- It is only as Stephen faces death as the first martyr that he sees a vision of Jesus standing at God's right hand (Acts 7:56).
- It is only when the apostle John is exiled to the island of Patmos that he gets to see a vision of the glorified Christ (Rev 1:13).

These believers experienced a fellowship with Christ in suffering that they had never experienced before. Does that mean you ought to seek out suffering? By no means. But it does mean that, when you experience suffering, you can expect to know Jesus in a way you've never known Him before.

> In suffering, you can expect to know Jesus as you never have before.

## Paul Finishes with a Song

Paul was a singer. Remember when he and Silas were beaten and imprisoned in Philippi? In that situation, I think I would be moaning and complaining, but not Paul. Acts 16:25 says, "About midnight Paul and Silas were praying and singing hymns to God, and the other prisoners were listening to them." He was singing! Throughout his letters, scholars tell us that Paul often quoted pieces of ancient Christian hymns. His letters often include prayers called doxologies, which sometimes insert themselves right in the middle of a chapter. Apparently Paul would get so caught up in the truth he was writing that he would just break out singing praise to God right then, before moving on to his next point.

When my wife Katie and I were students in Bible college, a group students would go each Friday night to a local nursing home to visit t residents. That's where I met Raymond. My wife had known Raymd since she was a little girl. She could remember Raymond being wheeled into church every Sunday morning.

Raymond had multiple sclerosis. He was probably in his 40s when I met him. Raymond's mind was sharp, but he was a prisoner in his own body. He was confined to a bed, day after day in the nursing home, because he could not take care of himself.

Each Friday night, when Raymond would see us coming, a crooked smile would spread across his face. Katie and I would stand on either side of his bed and grab one of his hands, and through labored speech, every week Raymond would request that we would sing the same song with him. I had never heard the song before, but Katie and Raymond taught it to me. Every Friday, Raymond would smile and sing:

> *I'm so happy, I'm so happy*
> *I'm so happy, happy, happy, happy, happy, happy, happy*
> *I'm so happy, I'm so happy*
> *'Cause Jesus is a friend of mine.*

I never ceased being amazed. Raymond lay there locked up in his own body, day after endless day, yet he could sing with joy because of Jesus. What faith!

Paul was just like Raymond. In the midst of physical pain, heartbreak, loneliness, and loss, Paul could still sing because he sensed the companionship of Jesus. At the end of this letter of 2 Timothy, Paul knows Jesus is near and writes, "The Lord will rescue me from every evil attack and will bring me safely to his heavenly kingdom." Do you know what the next line 'n 2 Timothy 4:18 is?

It's a doxology: "To him be glory for ever and ever. Amen." Paul goes t *singing.*

That's finish-line faith.

Remember the Big Jake Principle from chapter one: *It's not how you start ce that matters. It's how you finish.* When you feel tired and weary and read through this book of 2 Timothy again. Let the Spirit-inspired of Paul breathe new life into your soul. May you sense the presence close at your side, and may you sing with joy because you know a friend of mine."

no matter what happens: don't quit.

**111**

C
O
N
C
L
U
S
I
O
N
sus